CONCILIUM

CONCILIUM 2001/3

THE ECUMENICAL CONSTITUTION OF CHURCHES

Edited by

José Oscar Beozzo and Giuseppe Ruggieri

SCM Press · London

Published by SCM Press, 9–17 St Albans Place, London N1

ISBN: 0 334 03064 1

Printed by Biddles Ltd, Guildford and King's Lynn

Concilium Published February, April, June, October,
December

Contents

Introduction: Towards an Ecumenical Structuring of the Churches.
An Invitation to Recognize the Unity in Process
    JOSÉ OSCAR BEOZZO and GIUSEPPE RUGGIERI   7

I. Structures of Communion before the Great Divisions

The Local Church in the Universal Communion of the Churches
according to Ancient Canon Law
    DIMITRI SALACHAS   21

The Priority of the Preaching of the Word of God, the Liturgy and
Diaconia over Doctrine
    HANS-JOACHIM SCHULZ   34

Patterns of *Koinonia* in the First Christian Centuries
    ANGELO DI BERARDINO   45

II. Practical Perspectives

'Hierarchy of Truths' – and Ecumenical Praxis
    OTTO HERMANN PESCH   59

Towards an Ecumenical Interpretation of the Code of Canon Law of the
Latin Catholic Church
    ALPHONSE BORRAS   74

Ecumenical Openings in the Code of Canons of the Eastern Churches
    ASTRID KAPTIJN   86

Patterns of Synodality Today
    PIERRE VALLIN   99

The Paradigm of Assisi
 FAUSTINO TEIXERA   111

Ecumenical Gestures in Contemporary Catholicism
 ALBERTO MELLONI   121

The Petrine Ministry as Service of the 'Pilgrim Churches'
 GIUSEPPE ALBERIGO   136

Documentation
Reactions to *Dominus Iesus* in the German–Speaking World
 CHRISTINE VAN WIJNBERGEN   147

Contributors   153

Introduction: Towards an Ecumenical Structuring of the Churches

An Invitation to Recognize the Unity in Process

JOSÉ OSCAR BEOZZO AND GIUSEPPE RUGGIERI

Christians today evaluate the progress of the churches towards unity in a variety of ways, and their assessments range from pessimism to optimism. By contrast, this issue of *Concilium* offers an invitation to an open realism, or an invitation to recognize what is *possible now* and what at the same time, to the degree to which it has been effectively implemented, will allow further progress to be made.

In doing this, however, the contributors to this issue do not want to retrace the progress of theological dialogue between the various churches. This is not because they fail to appreciate the great progress that has been made in understanding the divergent positions on problems which have been, and still are, serious factors in the divisions between the churches, ranging from the understanding of scripture and tradition to the doctrine of justification, the sacraments and in particular ministry in the church. Rather they want to distance themselves to some degree from the 'exclusive' privilege given to the dialogue over doctrine. While such a dialogue is always legitimate and necessary, it in fact runs two risks if it is not set in a broader context, that brings out not only the doctrinal dimension of faith but all the other elements of church life.

The first risk is that the theological and doctrinal dialogue becomes a surrogate for the way towards unity. One sometimes gets the impression that everything can be said, from the creed without the *filioque* to the recognition of a substantial accord on the doctrine of justification, provided that there are no changes in the structure of the churches as they are now and provided that nothing disturbs the jealous defence of their 'confessional identity'.

The second risk is the opposite one, of supposing that doctrinal consensus can of itself lead to reconciliation between the churches. But just as it was not only – or sometimes not even mainly – doctrinal motives which led to the divisions in the churches, so too we may expect that equally the overcoming of doctrinal differences is not in itself enough to lead towards unity.

In this connection our intention is not to propose new ways, but simply to reaffirm shared convictions which nevertheless remain purely theoretical achievements, without having any effect in practice. It is, for example, recognized at the highest level of the churches concerned that the cause of the division between the churches acknowledged in the fourth century by the Council of Ephesus on the one hand and the Nestorian churches on the other was not doctrine as such. Thus on 11 November 1994 Pope John Paul II and the patriarch of the Assyrian Church of the East (Nestorian by tradition) signed a joint declaration in which they proclaimed 'before the world' their common faith in the mystery of the incarnation of the Word of God, true God and true man.

> The humanity to which the blessed Virgin Mary gave birth was always that of the Son of God himself. This is the reason why the Assyrian Church of the East prays to the Virgin Mary as 'the Mother of Christ our God and Saviour'. In the light of the same faith the Catholic tradition addresses Mary as 'Mother of God' and hence as 'Mother of Christ'. We both acknowledge the legitimacy and rightness of these expressions of the same faith and respect the preference of each church in its life and in its liturgical piety. *This is the only faith that we profess in the mystery of Christ. The controversies of the past have led to anathemas regarding persons and formulae. Today the Spirit of the Lord allows us better to understand how the divisions which arose in this way were largely due to failures of understanding.*[1]

That means that while the doctrinal divergences are not annulled, today they appear in a new light. The problem then is that of knowing what it is today that allows us to see these doctrinal differences in a new light, which is no longer dramatic or explosive. A similar question can be put to the agreement between Catholics and Lutherans on the doctrine of justification.

Evidently the answer is to be sought in an analysis of the historical context which led to what we would now judge to be an excessive importance being attached to doctrinal formulations. And with as much evidence, we have to ask ourselves whether today other doctrinal differences which were also considered cause of divisions are still so, for the same or for other reasons.

However, attempting such a task would also take us away from the aims of this issue. In a much more humble way it seeks to take a less ambitious, but nevertheless necessary course. The starting point is the conviction that the unity between the churches, though not complete, is already under way. In saying this we are talking not only of the unity *of the* church, of the dogmatic note that we profess in the creed which is common to Christians: I believe in *one* church. In fact all Christians who recognize themselves in the Niceno-Constantinopolitan creed believe that the unity of the church as the work of the Spirit is already present, but will not be fully manifested until the eschatological consummation.

Instead, we are talking about unity *between* the churches, even though this has not been fully implemented and has yet to be recognized sufficiently in practice: the one faith in Jesus Christ, the many and varied elements of Christian life, of worship, of doctrine and of discipline, even of scripture are already common in varying degrees to the Christian churches. These common elements allow us to speak of unity in process, even if it is not complete. The example given by the meeting in Toronto in May 2000 between Roman Catholic and Anglican bishops is a sign of the way in which the churches can recognize and increase this unity in process.[2]

Towards an ecumenical structuring of the churches

Starting from this conviction, it seems important to focus attention on the effective 'structure/structuring' of the churches in such a way that their character as churches is recognized or there is reconciliation of their diversities. However, it is necessary to clarify the meaning of the terms 'structure/structuring', particularly so that it is not understood in a mainly sociological sense. In his *Vocabulaire technique et critique de la philosophie*,[3] Lalande gave three meanings to the term 'structure'. The first is that of a 'disposition of the parts which form a whole, as opposed to their functions', a meaning which occurs above all in physics and biology; the second is that of a 'whole formed of phenomena in harmony as opposed to a simple combination of elements, in such a way that every phenomenon depends on the others and is what it is only within its relationship with the others and thanks to them'; the third meaning, analogous to the previous one, is that of an 'overall orientation which dominates a mentality and organizes it around a given idea of directive value'.

It is clear that here we are referring to the second sense of the term, though freeing it from its connections with Gestalt psychology which have governed it historically. In fact in a theological reflection the structure cannot be seen only from the punctual and synchronic, almost static, perspective of a single form. The church is a reality which is always in movement, whose faithfulness to its identity is guaranteed by the Spirit. Hence the structure itself can vary over time, but that does not alter the fact that as a permanent datum it has an internal structural logic, a disposition, an order, which functions for the well-being of all. The adjective 'ecumenical', added to structuring or structure, then seeks to indicate what logic of church unity makes it possible, by incarnating it in a precise 'order', in a precise 'disposition' of church life, to respect the unity already given to the churches and at the same time to be open to a more complete realization of this unity.

In this connection it is useful to refer to the original meaning of 'hierarchy', which in the writings of Dionysius the Areopagite indicates the gradual communication of God through which there are 'grades' with an internal arrangement, corresponding to the economy of salvation, of this self-giving by God to human beings. This disposition has to be recognized in the church. Before the term hierarchy (sacred origin, sacred order, sacred lordship) underwent a change, from the Middle Ages onwards, so that it came to denote the various degrees of the power of order and the different grades of jurisdiction, it had the meaning, taken from Neoplatonism, of an ordered structure of worldly and Christian reality which has its origin in God himself.[4] The theme of the 'hierarchy of truths', which is taken up many times in this issue, cannot be understood without this reference.

Thus 'structuring/structure' is meant to indicate the translation of this disposition, the logic inherent in the communication by God to human beings, into action, and the 'ecumenical structuring/structure of the churches' means the will to make manifest, specifically in respect of the ordered whole of the elements which constitute the life of the church, God's intention, revealed in Jesus of Nazareth, that all should be one as he and the Father are one.

Having defined the meaning of the term which is meant to indicate the common intentions of the contributions in this issue of *Concilium*, it remains to spell out some important questions of method.

The first relates to the sapiential (meaning that it is not simply the fruit of theological ingenuity) and spiritual (i.e. in obedience to the Spirit) character of any ecumenical ecclesial structuring. In the century which has just passed it was John XXIII who showed this capacity for bringing out the internal logic of ecclesial life. This pope, who was far removed from being a professional theologian, and also from being one of those who are often called 'progressives', and very close to the wisdom of the church fathers because he personally spent a good deal of time reading them, had the wisdom to demonstrate the living character of church doctrine over against the fixity of neoscholastic theology. He laid bare what here we call structure, using terms like '*aggiornamento*' and 'pastoral magisterium', and thus indicated the need for the 'living substance' of the gospel to be transmitted in means adequate to the times, so as to usher in the 'new Pentecost' of the church. *Aggiornamento* was not an alternative to faithfulness; it was not the abandonment of the 'immutable' substance of the gospel but the expression of its living continuity in history.[5] The ecumenical structuring of the churches, seen as both a sapiental and a spiritual work, is thus not primarily a matter for professional theologians, but for all the people of God, which, in the variety of tasks and charisms, perceives the 'signs of the times' and the way that the Spirit is pointing out for the churches.

The second thing that has to be spelt out is the recurrent misunderstanding about our 'separations' or, if one wants to put it that way, about the lowest common denominator. The structuring of ecclesial life is not in fact a process of separating out an ecumenically pure 'nucleus' which all can use, as opposed to an accidental 'core' which belongs to the specific confessional character of the individual churches. In analogy to the clarifications made by contemporary theology in biblical hermeneutics, it is never possible to separate the substance of the message from its particular interpretation, since it is here that the substance of the message must always be grasped. Our specific individual and ecclesial nature is not an extraneous accident which can be separated from the grace which is given in common with the others, but the place where this grace is perceived, welcomed, and lived out. In that sense there are no definitive formulae here. And from this point of view the mystery of unity, which is already believed in, experienced and lived out in the churches, is present in their respective differences, provided that they adopt an attitude of humility and openness to the mystery of unity which does not allow itself to be circumscribed by them. Thus the myth of a lowest common denominator which has to be broadened and extended as far as possible so that all may come within it has to be abandoned. In fact, the opposite is the case, namely that the mystery of unity must be lived out from the differences themselves and within them. This means an 'ecumenical structuring' of the churches which remain different churches yet operate by increasingly being one church.

We conclude with a short account of the various contributions in this issue. We sum them up not in order to synthesize them, but to make clear what was asked of the various contributors.

The sense of the reference to the past

The first part of the issue is devoted to the 'structures of communion before the great divisions'. The spirit which presides over this examination of the past is not the 'classic' one which idealizes the first centuries of church history and thinks that it is possible today simply to revive the forms of the past. History leaves nothing untouched.

There are various reasons for this examination of the past. It can be explained in two ways. First, to speak of an ecumenical structuring of the churches today, and hence of the adaptation of the forms of ecclesial life to the needs of a 'sorority' of the churches who live out their own diversity in a 'reconciled' way, is not simply a utopia or a dream. In the past the structuring of the churches was more open than it is now. And if we are to obey the principle of realism, we cannot move forward without any real point of reference; it is important to see how much is given in the church.

Secondly, this examination of the past aims to challenge the validity of a hermeneutical principle which today is almost universally accepted and which was expressed effectively by Joseph Ratzinger in a lecture in Graz in 1976: 'Although it is illegitimate here to silence history and to retrace the course of the centuries, it is legitimate to affirm today that what has been possible for a millennium cannot be impossible for Christians today.'[6]

Then it is important that for centuries the church has known the structural primacy of the local church over the universal church (cf. the article by D. Salachas). It is also important that the status of doctrine in the church was different, in that doctrine was not autonomous but substantially ordered by and subordinated to preaching and worship (cf. the article by Hans-Joachim Schulz). Finally, it is important that in the first Christian centuries the channels of communication were much more dynamic (visits and letters, synods determined by territory, etc.) and less constrained by a monolithic recognition of a single discipline (cf. the article by Angelo Di Berardino).

Today the structural primacy of the local church seems to be one of the vital conditions for an ecumenical structuring of the churches. This is so for two sets of reasons. First, it alone allows the conception and practice of the unity of the church as 'unity in communion'. This involves reflection on the mystery of the Trinity itself, a traditional motive, as is demonstrated in Salachas' article. The unity of the church, nourished by communion with the eucharistic body of Christ, does not correspond to the sociological and juridical models tried out in the social sphere, but rather reflects the mystery of the divine life which is communion in plurality and plurality in communion. If any other analogy can be affirmed, it can only be that of the unity between husband and wife.

But there is another important aspect which only the structural primacy of the local church makes it possible to respect. The late J. M. Tillard loved to emphasize it: precisely because the local church is rooted in a territory, it is 'the human (geographical, cultural, historical, sociological) space where the gospel of God – "fulfilled" at Jerusalem in the resurrection of Christ and at Pentecost, which liberated its effects – grasped the whole of *homo* (man) and the *humus* (ground) in which he germinates, *homo qua humus*, *homo* and *humus*.[7] It is the concrete, historical character of grace, which is always grace for someone in a particular place and at a particular moment of history, that comes to manifest itself in the structural primacy of the local church. Hence diversity, lived out in communion, is truly a testimony to the 'multi-coloured' divine wisdom (cf. Eph. 3.10).

On the other hand this primacy of the local church must not be mis-understood so that the vision of the local church is made the alternative to the universal church. As W. Kasper has recently asserted, to say that the one church is given in the local churches and from these (*in quibus et ex quibus*) does not mean that the universal church is the sum and the result of the local churches, just as the local churches are not provinces and articulations of the one universal church. The one church is a gift of God and not the result of human action from below. It is the fruit of the unity of the Father, the Son and the Spirit, who give themselves in every local church, above all in its supreme activity, the celebration of the eucharist. The local church and the universal church interpenetrate each other in turn. To affirm an ontological and chronological primacy of the universal church over the local churches is not a compulsory way of affirming this character of the one church as grace.[8]

We intend the necessary integration and subordination of the doctrinal dimensions to preaching and liturgical celebration, a topic dealt with in Schultz's article, to be seen as a way of playing down the doctrinal conflict between the churches, since in fact they converge much more closely in the faith, in preaching and in worship. But to play down this doctrinal diversity does not mean relativizing Christian truth. In fact it is important to distinguish between doctrine and truth. Doctrine is one of the forms in which the truth is expressed, which is grasped more deeply in the church's confession. Moreover it is important, particularly in connection with an ecumenical structuring of the churches and an even more faithful recognition of the truth, to grasp that these aims do not have to be bound up with a controversialist form of proclamation of the truth.[9]

In fact there are also 'epochs' (in Heidegger's sense of the term) of Christian truth.[10] Believers 'wander' in its orbit, giving shape to representations of the truth which mark the segments of Christian time. These figures or 'wanderings' of the truth convey the toil of conversion to the Lord of those who have listened to his voice, the difficulty of 'submitting' the different human conceptualities to the adoration of the Crucified One.

Certainly an important work of disentanglement has been achieved when there is a move from the primacy of 'confession' and invocation to that of the 'determination of the truth'. This is the epoch particularly studied in Schultz's article.

Another 'epoch', another 'wandering' in the orbit of Christian truth was that of the rise of theology as 'science'.[11] In this way the new urban culture was integrated into Christian knowledge. But this operation contained within itself a risk to which subsequent generations did not pay sufficient attention: the loss of the connotation of knowledge of the truth as an experience made possible by the sense of communion with Christ.[12] In later theological reflection the truth would be thought of under the 'burden of the schism'[13] between the doctrinal theological element and the experience of communion with Christ, the Christian life in its spiritual dimension. Thus theologians almost completely lost sight of the fact that 'the full concept of truth offered by the gospel consists only in the living representation of theory in praxis, of knowledge in action. "If you keep my word . . . you will know the truth" (John 8.32)'.[14]

Finally, it is necessary here to refer to another 'epoch' of truth, that which culminates in the modern Catholic concept of dogma. This is a product of the division of the Western church. The most significant feature of the conception of truth now does not lie in the determination of its content but in the determination of its genesis, the way in which it can be obtained. 'In other words, the reply to the question of what a dogma is, is determined by the reply to the question of what can become a dogma within the Catholic Church.'[15] And in this way an answer developed above all in the climate of the anti-Protestant controversy, through Stapleton, Bellarmine, Gotti and others. The so to speak 'ultimate' definition of dogma in modern Catholic theology which was then taken up by Vatican I was that of Philipp Nero Chrismann, who, influenced by the Jesuit François Veron, said that the 'dogma of faith is none other than a doctrine or a truth revealed by God which is proposed to be believed in with (an act of) divine faith through a public judgment of the church in such a way that the contrary doctrine is condemned as heretical'. [16] In other words, here the truth is conceived of as a defence of one's own specific character (the authority of 'public judgment', i.e. that of the magisterium of the Catholic Church) with a view to marking out heresy. A concept of truth as a boundary aimed at marking out what differentiates one from others emerges here. But this concept is possible only in the context of a break in communion and has the function of maintaining this break.

The material presented in the last of the articles relating to the past (Di Bernardino) is more functional; again our intention is that it should differentiate between the ministries and the channels of unity in the church. Our age, with its increased speed of communication, here runs the risk of doing away with this multiplicity of times and procedures which served to resolve conflicts in the early church. This obliteration of such features closely resembles that brought about by the excessive Roman centralization in the second millennium.

Practical prospects

The second part of this issue is devoted to 'practical prospects'. The attempt here is to show how some achievements are waiting to be put into practice, and how it is possible to recognize the unity in process.

However, in this respect first of all we have to point out a gap in this issue. The author contacted to discuss 'the faith expressed in the worship of the churches as the greatest factor in their divisions' failed to produce his article. It did seem to us that this was an important topic in understanding what is called the 'ecumenical structuring of the churches'. This is not in fact an unrealistic programme, but primarily a recognition of what exists. This was an aspect which was very dear to that great ecumenical theologian E. Schlink, who emphasized among 'the fundamental structures of universal unity' at least two facts which we do well to remember by quoting directly from his *magnum opus*:[17]

1. Since Jesus Christ, in the power of the Holy Spirit, is truly present and gives himself in the liturgy of every local church, the local church does not come into being through the sum of the local churches but is a reality in every local church. 2. The unity of the universal church does not consist in the quality of its confessional formula, its liturgical order and its ministries, but in the fact that every church with its confession and in the ordering of its liturgy and its ministries serves the one Lord of the church.

The invitation to look hopefully at other communities, without limiting oneself to dogmatic affirmations, but taking into account the global features of their life, liturgy, testimony, piety and so on, was therefore in accord with these premises.

If worship, what could be called the concrete presence of the Spirit of the Risen Christ in the midst of believers, is one of the main places in which the unity which is in process of the churches, despite the differences, can be recognized, we must not forget the other achievements: Vatican II's conviction of a hierarchy of truths arising from the relationship between the foundation and the end on the one hand, and the means on the other (O. H. Pesch); the ecumenical openings made possible by the new legal Codes of the Catholic Church, above all in the light of the new ecumenical Directory of 1993 (A. Borras and A. Kaptijn); and the presence in the actual practices of the churches, including the Catholic Church, of a synodicality which involves not only the bishops but all the believing people, if only in an initial and timid way (P. Vallin).

Alongside these achievements we need to record others, of a rather different kind, those which consist of 'actions'. The term 'actions' appears in a central passage of the Vatican II constitution *Dei Verbum,* 2, where it is said that the economy of the divine revelation is realized in 'actions and words'. The reference of this sentence was to the celebration of the sacrament, where the symbolic actions, together with the words which accompany them, are meant to denote the *res,* the reality for which the celebration is ordained.[18] In history these are the actions in which, in a way analogous to what happens in the celebration of the sacraments, the Spirit makes possible a communication from God to human beings. It is no exaggeration to see the World Day of Prayer for Peace held at Assisi in October 1986 (cf. the article by F. Teixera in this issue) as one of these actions. In our view Assisi remains an action the whole richness of which has still to be understood. In Assisi an event which was somehow paradoxical took place.

Without going so far as a common prayer for peace, the representatives of the religions all prayed at the same time and in the same mode of space, for the same aim, peace, but following the canons, rites and contents of the religious tradition which was proper to each of them. The diversity was thus transformed into a network of common actions, aimed at making something sacred and intangible of the diversity. And all this was on the initiative of the Bishop of Rome.

However, Assisi has not been the only action in which a positive recognition of diversity has appeared. It was directed towards religious diversity as such. But the papacy of John XXIII and the council inaugurated a series of actions in an opposite sense to those predominating in the great season of enmity between the churches, above all in the second Christian millennium, by means of which a communion between the churches greater than that 'formally' recognized in doctrine was recognized. What 'theological' weight do these actions have? That is the question which runs through the article by A. Melloni.[19]

Finally, the theme of the Petrine service had to be included in this issue. By common recognition, shared also by Paul VI and the current Bishop of Rome, the papacy is one of the main obstacles on the way to the achievement of a visible unity of the Christian churches. However, John Paul II has also invited not only Catholics but also other Christians to rethink the mode in which the Petrine service is exercised. So recognizing unity in process in the churches implies welcoming this invitation. As such it is a grace given today to all the churches. Thus looking forward to new forms in which the Petrine ministry can be exercised (cf. G. Alberigo's article) is a course which must be taken to bring about an ecumenical structuring of the churches.

An omen

The publication of the document *Dominus Iesus* has set all Christians talking. Even some circles of the Roman Curia have expressed their perplexity. So here we have made room for a documentation on the reception of the document, above all in the German-speaking world.

It has been rightly observed that, taken one by one, all the affirmations of *Dominus Iesus* can be derived literally from one or other of the texts of Vatican II. And it can also be recognized that it is right, when confronted with so many flights forward, to affirm some convictions, albeit with exasperation. But this document seems to lack above all a recognition of what the Spirit has brought about in the churches over the past decades, in the power of the conciliar event which should have been read in the sense of inspiration which governs it. A recognition of the event cannot be limited to formal admissions but must be understood as a joyful adherence to what the Spirit is saying to the churches. The omen is thus that the dialectic which this document maintains is a useful summons to an even greater welcome to the greatness of God in history.

Translated by John Bowden

Notes

1. *Osservatore Romano*, 12 November 1994, our emphasis.
2. Cf. above all the review by J-M. R. Tillard in *Il Regno documenti* 45, 2000, pp.596–600.
3. Paris 1947.
4. Cf. R. Roques, *L'univers dionysien. Structure hiérarchique du monde selon le Pseudo-Denys*, Paris 1954.
5. Cf. G. Alberigo, 'Teologia fra tradizione e rinnovamento nel magistero del patriarca Roncalli', in *Angelo Giuseppe Roncalli. Dal patriarcato di Venezia alla cattedra di San Pietro*, ed V. Branca and S. Rosso-Mazzinghi, Florence 1985, pp.15–28; G. Pattaro, 'La "teologia" che ispira il pensiero pastoral del cardinale Roncalli a Venezia', ibid., pp.149–55; G. Ruggieri, 'Appunti per una teologia in

papa Roncalli', in *Papa Giovanni*, ed G. Alberigo, Rome and Bari 1987, pp.245–71. For an overall view cf. already G. Lercaro, 'Linee per una ricerca su Giovanni XXIII', in *Per la forza dello Spirito. Discorsi conciliari del card. Giacomo Lercaro*, produced by the Institute for Religious Sciences, Bologna 1984, pp.267–310.

6. Now in J. Ratzinger, *Theologische Prinzipienlehre. Bausteine zur Fundamental-theologie*, Munich 1982, p.209. Because of what we have said above, we shall not refer here to the further remarks in id., *Kirche, Ökumene, Politik*, Einsiedeln 1987, pp.76ff., 81ff., on the misunderstandings to be avoided in the under-standing of this formula, almost as if it wanted to propose an ecumenism of a return to the past.

7. J.-M. R. Tillard, *L'Église locale. Ecclésiologie de communion et catholicité*, Paris 1995, p.53.

8. W. Kasper, 'Das Verhältnis von Universalkirche und Ortskirche. Freund-schaftliche Auseinandersetzung mit der Kritik von Joseph Kardinal Ratzinger', *Stimme der Zeit* 218, 2000, pp.795–804. But see also Ratzinger's own reaction, 'Die grosse Gottesidee "Kirche" ist keine Schwärmerei', *Frankfurter All-gemeine Zeitung*, 22 December 2000.

9. For a broader treatment of this subject than is possible here cf. G. Ruggieri, 'La verità crocifissa fra Trinità e storia. Per una determinazione del rapporto tra verità e comunione', *Cristianesimo nella Storia* 16, 1995, pp.383–406.

10. G. Alberigo, 'Communione e verità', in *L'alterità. Concezioni ed esperienze nel cristianesimo contemporaneo*, ed A. Melloni and G. La Bella, Bologna 1995, pp.235–54, gives a brief synthesis of the development of the concept of truth at the Western Latin councils.

11. The basic study on the question is still that by M. D. Chenu. *La théologie comme science au XIIIe siècle*, Paris [3]1969.

12. It is enough to cite two classic studies to understand the difference in the theo-logy which developed as an alternative to monastic theology: M. Grabmann, *Geschichte der scholastischen Methode* (2 vols), Freiburg 1909, 1911; J. Leclercq, *Initiation aux auteurs monastiques du Moyen Age. L'amour des lettres et le désir de Dieu*, Paris [2]1957. It is even impossible to discover among the subjects discussed by Grabmann the central nuclei of monastic theology as these are presented by Leclercq: from *compunctio* to *otium*, from *simplicitas* to the *mea grammatica Christus* of Damian.

13. 'Die Last der Gezweiung': the expression comes from H. U. von Balthasar, 'Theologie und Heiligkeit', in *Verbum caro*, pp.195–225, esp.p.201.

14. Ibid.

15. G. Söll, *Dogma und Dogmenentwicklung*, HDG I/5, Freiburg, Basel and Vienna 1971, p.13.

16. *De fide divina*, Kempten 1792, §5; cf. Söll, *Dogma* (n.15), p.16.

17. E. Schlink, *Ökumenische Dogmatik. Grundzüge*, Göttingen 1983, p.559; but cf. above all his account of the value of liturgical reunion (ibid., pp.572–8).

18. Cf. H. de Lubac, 'Commentaire du préambule et du chapitre I', in B. D. Dupuy, *La révélation divine I: Constitution dogmatique Dei Verbum*, Paris 1968, pp.175–9.

19. Other topics which we were not able to discuss in this issue were those of 'The primacy of obedience to the Word of God and the confession of sin, with respect to the proclamation of identity', and 'Communion of the service of charity, of ministries, of preaching and the eucharistic table'.

I. Structures of Communion before the Great Divisions

The Local Church in the Universal Communion of the Churches according to Ancient Canon Law

DIMITRI SALACHAS

Preface

The church arose and exists in history as a local church. From the first centuries on, canon law broadly deals with the local church and its organization. The church which 'exists in' a particular place manifests itself as such when it is a 'community', an 'assembly', the elements of which – starting with the complex from which the church itself is built up, brought to life and grows – are determined by the New Testament: *koinonia* and *martyria* in faith, hope and love, *koinonia* and *martyria* in the sacraments, *koinonia* and *martyria* in the diversity of charisms, *koinonia* and *martyria* in reconciliation, *koinonia* and *martyria* in the ministry and in the care of all the churches. This *koinonia* and *martyria* is brought about through the work of the Holy Spirit. The church is fully the church when it is a eucharistic synaxis. That is why with the celebration of the Lord's eucharist in the individual local churches the church of God is built and grows, and with concelebration the communion between them is manifested (cf. Vatican II, UR 15).

The one and only church is identified with the *koinonia* of the local churches which celebrate the eucharist in the orthodoxy of the faith and in full ecclesial hierarchical communion. Thus the universal church is a *koinonia* made up of different local churches. The articulation and structure of this ecclesial and hierarchical communion among the local churches requires a juridical form animated by love to make it an 'organic reality'.

Starting from the structure of the local church, the experience of the local churches in the first millennium offers useful pointers.

I. The territorial principle of the local churches in the universality of the church

The territorial nature of the local churches which together form the universal church (*ten kata ten oikoumenen ekklesian*) follows from the information given in the New Testament and from normative early canon law. The local churches in which and from which the one and only Catholic church subsists are usually located within a particular territory, so that they comprise all the faithful who have their domicile in this territory. The church of Christ, one, holy, catholic and apostolic in its divine constitution, remains undivided and indivisible in its nature and essence as the mystery of salvation and communion, but in its reality and visible structure it presents itself as a divine institution with a dimension which is also earthly. In this aspect the church constitutes a pluralistic reality which can be divided, regrouped and territorially circumscribed.

The whole of ancient Christian ecclesiology developed around the 'local church', understood as the Christian community with the bishop as its head. The local churches of various geographical areas, with several bishops gathered round the chief of them, is a later development. The Council of Nicaea (325) tried to justify this development because it found it useful for safeguarding their unity and for organizational purposes. But neither at Nicaea nor later did the East lose sight of the local church with the bishop at its head. In its theological profile this 'Catholic' church is the body of Christ, of which the baptized are the members. The universal church is the communion of the local churches, and every bishop who has the care of his own local church, by virtue of this fact has the care of all the churches.

Canons 12 and 57 of the Synod of Laodicea (343/381) lay down that the bishops are ordained with a view to governing a local church. As a rule the territory of a local church coincided with a city. That also follows from canon 6 of the Synod of Sardica (343/344), according to which it is not generally permissible to ordain a bishop for a village or a small city, where a presbyter is sufficient, so as not to diminish the title and the authority of the bishop, but the bishops of the province must appoint bishops only in the cities. However, if the population of a city increases, so that it is considered worthy to be given a bishop, it is given one.

The canon establishes the main criterion for the founding of local churches and the institution of bishops. This is the pastoral care of the faithful, and not the vanity of presbyters ambitious to attain episcopal dignity. The bishop is a pastor of a portion of the people of God; a consistent number of faithful is required to constitute an episcopal see, and that is clearly the case in a variety of cities, larger or smaller. That is why in canons 12 and 17 the Council of Chalcedon establishes the principle of adapting ecclesiastical administration to civil administration: i.e. the elevation of the administrative status of a city entails the elevation of the status of the episcopal see and its bishop. In the sphere of a local church of the city entrusted to a bishop, smaller communities can be organized and entrusted to the pastoral care of presbyters; here the reference to territories, districts and small cities to be entrusted to the presbytery would be the origin of the institution of 'parish communities'. As a result the local 'episcopocentric' church soon developed into a communion of 'presbyterocentric communities'.

From this there follows the principle of the territoriality of the exercise of episcopal power and the prohibition against bishops infiltrating other territories. Therefore bishops exercise their power only within the confines of their own areas, so that order prevails in the church.

II. In every local church there is a single bishop, guarantor of its internal unity and its communion with the universal church

The structural primacy of the local churches is implemented and safeguarded by the ecclesiological and canonical principle that there is only one bishop in every local church. St Ignatius of Antioch (died 107) taught: 'Wherever the bishop appears let the congregation be present; just as wherever Jesus Christ is, there is the Catholic Church'; and again: 'See that you all follow the bishop, as Jesus Christ follows the Father, and the presbytery as if it were the apostles. And reverence the deacons as the command of God. Let no one do any of the things appertaining to the church without the bishop'; 'let that be considered a valid eucharist which is celebrated by the bishop or one whom he appoints'.[1] By means of his ordination the bishop is constituted minister in his local church, the church which he represents in the universal communion. In fact in the local church entrusted to the bishop, the church of Christ, one, holy, catholic and apostolic, is truly present and at work.

Consequently canon 8 of the Ecumenical Council of Nicaea I (325) lays down that 'there are not two bishops in the same city'. The authority of the bishop over his flock is such that two bishops cannot be tolerated in a single city. And the see of a metropolitan province cannot be occupied by two metropolitans.[2]

III. The bishop in his local church is the guardian of the orthodoxy of the universal church

As successors of the apostles, the bishops are responsible for communion in the apostolic faith and faithfulness to the demands of a life in accord with the gospel. The bishops to whom the care of a local church has been entrusted are defined as *in locum apostolorum a Christo positi*,[3] appointed by Christ in place of the apostles. To this degree they are guardians of the apostolic faith in their local church.

According to canon 80 of the Apostolic Canons (end of the third century) the bishop is 'master of the others' and therefore canon 12 of the Synod of Laodicea (343/381) lays down that the candidate for the episcopate must have his orthodoxy sufficiently tested in the judgment of the metropolitan and the neighbouring bishops. In electing and ordaining a bishop, the metropolitan and the bishops of the province express their judgment on the candidate whom before the Lord and the church of which he will be the pastor they consider to be more worthy and suitable than all the others; they are the witnesses before the church for which he is elected and ordained, for his sound faith, his good habits, his piety and zeal of spirit; they become witnesses to the faith of their churches and the faith of the newly elected bishop. With these guarantees the bishop becomes the guardian of the faith in his local church, of communion in the faith of the universal church, and the doctor and teacher of his people.

Canon 19 of the Trullan Council (691) orders the bishops to teach all the clergy and the people with the words of piety every day, and above all on Sundays, drawing from holy scripture the concepts and judgments of truth, without transgressing dogmas which have already been defined or departing from the traditions of the fathers. But when any question regarding scripture arises, it must be resolved in conformity with the writings of the holy fathers; rather than composing treatises out of their head they are to base themselves on the patristic writings.

IV. The bishop is the guardian of the ecclesial communion of his own church with the universal church

The unity of the local church is inseparable from the universal communion. The bond of ecclesiastical government has different levels extending as far as that of the universal church; in other words, ecclesiastical communion guarantees the unity of the church. According to canon 1 of the Ecumenical Council of Ephesus (431) the bishop who associates with heretics is excluded from ecclesiastical communion: the orthodox metropolitans and bishops of the province must see that this takes place. Canon 3 of the same council condemns those clergy who remain in communion with the separated bishops.

Canon 5 of the Ecumenical Council of Nicaea (325), which deals with the excommunicated and the obligation to hold synods twice a year, implicitly emphasizes the responsibility of each bishop to maintain the communion and the unity of his flock.

According to canon 10 of the Ecumenical Council of Chalcedon (451), clergy who separate from their bishops are suspended, and if they persist they are deposed.

According to canon 81 of the Synod of Carthage (419), the clergy must not commemorate the name of the bishop in the liturgy if he departs from ecclesiastical communion. Canon 13 of the first/second Council of Constantinople (861) establishes that the clergy, priests and deacons who depart from communion with their own bishop and do not commemorate his name in the divine liturgy are deposed. Canon 14 imposes the same penal sanction on the bishop with regard to his own metropolitan, and canon 15 on the metropolitan with regard to his own patriarch. The structure of the patriarchal Eastern churches seems clear in these three canons. Ecclesiastical communion is manifested in a particular way in the liturgical 'diptychs' (the book containing the names of the heads of the churches to be commemorated in the liturgy).

V. The synodical action of the bishops of the local churches

Just as the celebration of the eucharist as a whole makes the trinitarian ministry present, so the church in its institutions finds its model, its origin and its task in the mystery of the one God in three persons. Thus understood in the light of the mystery of the Trinity, the eucharist is the criterion for the functioning of all church life. The institutional elements should reflect visibly only the reality of the mystery of the Trinity.

Understood thus in the light of the mystery of the Trinity, the synodical action of the local bishops at different levels is in the image of the mystery of the Trinity and finds its ultimate foundation and model in that. Just as in the mystery of the Trinity the three persons are distinct without any diminution or subordination, so there is an order between the local churches and their bishops which does not affect their nature. The constitutive relationship of unity-multiplicity raises the question of the relationship between the authority inherent in any ecclesial institution and the conciliarity with which the mystery of the church as communion expresses itself at all levels.

In the course of history the church in East and West has known various ways in which communion between bishops is exercised, including the exchange of letters and visits from one church to another; however, the main form of communion is the synod or council. Especially in ecumenical councils which are gathered in the Holy Spirit in situations of crisis, the bishops of the church, with supreme authority, have made shared decisions in faith and issued canons to affirm the tradition of the apostles. According to the testimony of Irenaeus such communion guarantees the unity of doctrine and preaching of the churches, spread all over the world.[4] The historian L. Hertling defines this communion as a 'bond of union between the bishops and the faithful, bishops together and faithful together, which is made and manifested by eucharistic communion'.[5]

From the first centuries on there has been a distinction and a hierarchy (*taxis*) between the churches with an earlier foundation and the churches with a later foundation; between mother churches and daughter churches; between churches of major cities and more peripheral churches. This hierarchy soon found its conciliar expression formulated by the councils.

Different types of synods or local or regional councils of bishops have been organized in every region. Their forms have changed depending on places and eras, but their principle is to manifest and make effective the life of the church through the framework of the joint action of bishops under the presidency of the one who they recognize as being the first among them. In fact according to canon 34 of the Apostolic Canons, which is part of the canonical tradition of our church, the first of the bishops decides only in accord with the other bishops, and the latter do not decide anything of importance without the agreement of the former. The theme of primacy throughout the church and in particular the primacy of the Bishop of Rome can be approached from this perspective of communion among the local churches.[6] Obviously the primacy of the Bishop of Rome in the universal church is not just an institution of canonical ecclesiastical origin but corresponds to the will of Christ for his church, and therefore forms part of the divine constitution of the church.

The conciliar dimension of the church is realized at three levels of church life: (a) that of the local church entrusted to a bishop; (b) that of a group of local churches (provinces, patriarchates) with their bishops, who recognize who is first among them (metropolitan, patriarch); (c) that of the universal church with the whole episcopal body which recognizes its head, the first bishop of the Christian ecumene.

Canons 34 and 37 refer to the various local assemblies of bishops with their head. Canon 34 of the Apostolic Canons refers to the bishops of all nations and means rather the different ethnic, cultural and geographical areas, with various traditions, which Christianity has always known how to respect. This canon enunciates some principles of the synodical structure of the church.

The first bishop among the bishops of a province, a region or a patriarchate guarantees the unity of the local churches at these different levels and the canonical functioning of the synod. In the ancient conception of the church synodality and the primacy at different levels are two interdependent concepts.

Beyond doubt even before the first Ecumenical Council of Nicaea (325) the local churches of the same Roman province (*eparchia*) organized themselves around the mother city (*metropolis*) and its bishop, the metropolitan. The historian Eusebius speaks of the bishops who met 'by province' in synods for the controversy over the date of Easter.[7] The term 'eparchy' in the ancient canons denotes an institution which is already solidly established, i.e. the ecclesiastical province ('region' and also wider than that), whereas the term 'paroikia' denotes the local church ruled by the bishop. These 'provincial' synods are certainly the earliest in the church; they extend further and further until they include all the bishops of a 'nationality'. It is well known that many nationalities, i.e. peoples of different nations, lived together in the sphere of the Roman empire. Often the same Roman districts included more than one nationality and moreover the districts often changed.

First of all the canon guarantees the autonomy of the 'dioceses', a term which in Roman law denotes broad areas of civil administration instituted by the Emperor Diocletian (there were fifteen throughout the Roman empire at the end of the fourth century). In keeping with this concept, in ecclesiastical law 'diocese' denotes vast ecclesiastical areas composed of many provinces. The bishops of the five great dioceses are subsequently given the title 'patriarch'. However, the patriarch must respect the autonomy of the provinces which in Roman law are called 'eparchies'. The canon confirms the decisions of Nicaea I about the treatment of the affairs of an ecclesiastical province by its own synod. The heads of the provinces, i.e. the metropolitans, continue to be elected by the bishops of the province, but the patriarch has the right to ordain them (cf. canon 28 of the Council of Chalcedon, 451; canon 15 of the first-second Synod of Constantinople, 861). Therefore the relations between patriarch and metropolitan are regulated in accordance with the same principle as the relations between metropolitan and bishops. It is again the same principle of conciliarity, inspired by canon 34 of the Apostolic Canons, which expresses the unity of the church. The patriarch is the symbol and minister of the unity of the patriarchal churches, just as the metropolitan is the symbol and minister of the unity of the metropolitan church.

Canon 8 of the Ecumenical Council of Ephesus (431) lays down that the ancient laws and customs of each province shall be kept pure and intact.

This canon refers to the legitimate claims of the bishops of the church of Cyprus over against those of the bishop of Antioch, and sanctions the principle of episcopal synodicality, which is expressed in the right of each metropolitan to autonomous rule. So this is not an innovation; the principle is an ancient one, already in force before the Council of Nicaea (325). The two first ecumenical councils simply recognized the synodical institution of each province. Consequently the canon recognizes the right of each metropolitan to claim his autonomy from the supreme authority of the church, when this is infringed by anyone.

The principle of synodicality and of communion among the local churches applies particularly in the designation of bishops. The ordination of a bishop is one of the 'questions' which transcend the authority of an individual bishop, and involves more bishops. It is a matter of choosing pastors who will ensure the faithful transmission of the deposit of faith and salvation received from Christ. Canon 4 of the Council of Nicaea I (325) deals explicitly with the 'constitution' (*katastasis* = institution) of the bishops, which includes canonical election and ordination, calling for the presence of all the bishops of the province and canonical ratification by the metropolitan of the canonical election made by the synod.[8]

The genuine Eastern canonical tradition sanctions the principle of synodicality, which is inseparable from that of the primacy at various levels: province, patriarchate, universal church. In connection with the different types of primacy we need to note:

The axiom '*primus inter pares*' used to define the role of the bishop of Rome in the ecclesiology of the Orthodox churches is well known. Beyond doubt in the sacramental sphere there is nothing in the church which is hierarchically superior to the episcopate; therefore all bishops are '*pares*' in the episcopate and the '*primus*' among them is '*primus inter pares*'. But the term '*primus*' at the different levels of the organization of the church has some theological and canonical significance in the tradition of the undivided church. In fact the Eastern patriarchs also had rights which other bishops did not have, and these evidently did not derive directly from the power of ordination,[9] but were *iure canonica*. The prerogatives of honour (*ta presbeia times*) attributed in the church to the '*protos*' were meant to acknowledge a function, a ministry, a service, and bear witness to the respect which was owed to him.[10] When this axiom was applied to the bishop of the church of Rome, founded by Peter and Paul, who presides over charity and is the cause of his *potentior principalitas*,[11] the early church wanted to recognize in the Bishop of Rome a distinctive authority among the bishops of the universal church, aimed at ensuring unity and communion. The episcopal college grouped around the *protos* of the bishops, especially in the ecumenical council, like the bishop of Rome exercised the same power, in two different modes: the collegial and synodical mode, the personal and primatial mode of the Bishop of Rome. These two modes of exercising power are inseparable in the spirit of canon 34 of the Apostolic Canons.[12]

VI. The autonomy of the Eastern churches in the unity of the universal church

The concept of the universal church, of the *varietas ecclesiarum* and their autonomy, with specific reference to the patriarchal churches, is described in the Vatican II Dogmatic Constitution on the Church, LG 23d:

> It has come about through divine providence that, in the course of time, different churches set up in various places by the apostles and their successors joined together in a multiplicity of organically united groups which, whilst safeguarding the unity of the faith and the unique divine structure of the universal church, have their own discipline, enjoy their own liturgical usage and inherit a theological and spiritual patrimony. Some of these, notably the ancient patriarchal churches, as mothers in the faith, gave birth to other daughter-churches, as it were, and down to our own days they are linked with these by bonds of a more intimate charity in what pertains to the sacramental life and in a mutual respect for rights and obligations. This multiplicity of local churches, unified in a common effort, shows all the more resplendently the catholicity of the undivided church.

This text, which is of particular doctrinal importance, cites in a note as the main canonical source of the institution of the ancient patriarchal churches first of all canons 6 and 7 of the first Ecumenical Council of Nicaea (325); this is an institution of divine law recognized by the first ecumenical councils. The council text does not attribute their origin to an express will of Christ, so that it is not part of the divine constitution of the church, but a disposition of divine providence to further ecclesiastical communion. To maintain communion at different regional levels, in both the East and the West there was reliance on the episcopal sees founded, according to tradition, by the apostles or by one of their immediate colleagues. This kind of division into more or less broad territorial regions does not damage in any way the unity of the faith or the fundamental divine constitution of the universal church. The text speaks above all of the ancient patriarchal churches without making express reference to the East or to the West.

The Conciliar Decree on the Catholic Eastern Churches, OE no.5, spells out the solemn affirmations mentioned:

> This Council solemnly declares that the churches of the East like those of the West have the right and duty to govern themselves according to their own special disciplines. For these are guaranteed by ancient tradition, and seem to be better suited to the customs of their faithful and to the good of their souls.

The same principle is confirmed for the Eastern Orthodox churches, whose right to internal autonomy of direct right to self-rule according to their own disciplines is explicitly recognized by the council (UR 16).

'The right and duty to govern themselves according to their own special disciplines' presuppose their own superior internal authority, or in legislative, administrative and judicial matters, provided that the supreme authority of the church is maintained which, according Catholic ecclesiology, is exercised by the Roman Pontiff and the bishops in communion with him; the college of bishops, whose head is the Roman pontiff and whose members are the bishops, exercises in solemn form power over the universal church in the ecumenical council. Consequently, 'the right and duty to govern themselves according to their own special disciplines' comprises the right to have their own canonical, common and particular norm.

All this indicates that the *ecclesia universa* consists in the communion of the different churches of East and West, above all those matrices of the faith founded on the apostles and their successors, which are governed by their own norms.

During the first and second millennia, the church of Rome was always aware that its bishop, Peter's successor, had a ministry of universal communion and unity. The difference was that that in the first millennium, during which the church was undivided, the bishop of Rome exercised his ministry in the sense set out in the conciliar document *Unitatis Redintegratio* no.14: for a millennium Christians were united 'through a brotherly communion of faith and sacramental life. If disagreements in faith and discipline arose among them, the Roman See occupied by common consent a moderator (*sede romana moderante*)'. However, in the second millennium, while the bishop remained convinced that by the will of God he possessed the ministry of unity, the church was no longer *de facto* in the state in which it had been in the first millennium. In the second millennium a break in ecclesiastical communion between East and West developed and persisted, as from the fifteenth century on, following the Reformation, did a break between the Catholic church and the Protestant churches. Neither the non-Catholic East nor the non-Catholic West put in question the particular ministry of the Bishop of Rome, but this was now in a different context, namely of non-communion with, of *de facto* separation from, Rome. For the East the norm and experience of the first ecumenical councils remained firm: these recognize in the Bishop of Rome the first bishop in the universal communion of the churches. In the Eastern churches the institution of the 'pentarchy' remained firm along with the prerogatives of honour (*ta presbeia times*) among the great churches of the Christian ecumene: Rome, Constantinople Alexandria, Antioch, Jerusalem, patriarchal sees, mothers of the churches in the East and in the West. The Bishop of Rome is 'the first bishop in order and in honour'; that implies a ministry, an authoritative and authentic function, to be exercised as a diaconia, an irreplaceable service through the will of Christ. That means that if full communion is re-established, the churches which are not now in full communion with the Catholic church will recognize in the Bishop of Rome his function as the 'moderator' who expresses, safeguards, guarantees and confirms the unity of the universal church. The episcopal college of the Christian ecumene would rediscover its cohesion and its normal and canonical foundation here, especially if this college exercised the power of the ecumenical council over the universal church in a solemn way.

Even after the break in ecclesiastical communion between East and West, the church of Rome, while affirming the primacy – by the will of Christ – of its bishop, Peter's successor, among the churches of the Christian ecumene, sanctioned the principle of the patriarchal institution and of the 'pentarchy', renewing the ancient privileges of the patriarchal sees: after the Roman church the church of Constantinople has first place, that of Alexandria second, that of Antioch third, and that of Jerusalem fourth, the dignity of each remaining firm.[13]

It remains important to emphasize that 'the successor of Peter, that is the bishop of the apostolic church of Rome, who "presides in love" as St Ignatius of Antioch puts it, is in the midst of those who presided over the ancient patriarchal churches',[14] as these are described in LG 23. In maintaining and guaranteeing the unity of the universal church, the Bishop of Rome recognizes that he has a specific and unique service of love for this cause, which was the object of Christ's prayer on the eve of his passion.

The Greek Orthodox professor Vlassios Phidas, in his analysis of the authority of the Bishop of Rome during the first millennium as '*primus*' among the patriarchs of the 'pentarchy' (Rome, Constantinople, Alexandria, Antioch and Jerusalem), i.e. of the *prima sedes*, concludes that this authority was not a simple and theoretical honour but had an essential and real ecclesiastical function for the service of the unity of the universal church in faith and canonical order.[15]

Conclusion

The Second Vatican Council in UR 16 solemnly declared that from earliest times the churches of the East followed their own disciplines, endorsed by the holy fathers and the councils, including the ecumenical councils. So it declared that the churches of the East, mindful of the necessary unity of all the churches, have the right to govern themselves in accordance with their own disciplines, as being more in keeping with the nature of their faithful and more suitable in providing for the good of souls.

The one and only church identifies itself with the *koinonia* and *martyria* of the local churches in faith, hope and love, communion in the sacraments, communion in the diversity of charisms in reconciliation and in ministry. The agent of this *koinonia* and *martyria* is the Spirit of the Risen Lord. The communion of every local church is not only with the neighbouring churches but also with all the local churches present in the world. All the bishops are responsible for the 'care of all the churches' (II Cor. 11.28) as members of the episcopal college which succeeded the college of the apostles, with the Bishop of Rome, Peter's successor, at their head. This universal dimension of their episcopate (vigilance, supervision) is inseparable from the particular dimension of the offices entrusted to them. In the case of the Bishop of Rome the 'care of all the churches' acquires particular force because it is part of his ministry instituted by the will of Christ.

Translated by John Bowden

Notes

1. *To the Smyrnaeans* 8.1–2.
2. Cf. canon 12 of the Ecumenical Council of Chalcedon (451).
3. Cf. canon 1 of Gennadius, patriarch of Constantinople.
4. Irenaeus, *Adversus haereses* I, 10,2.
5. L. Hertling, *Communio*, Rome 1961, 5.
6. Cf. the Joint International Commission for the Theological Dialogue between the Catholic Church and the Orthodox Church, Valamo Document (1988).
7. Eusebius of Caesarea, *Church History* V, 23, 2–3.
8. Cf. J. Gaudemet, *L'Eglise dans l'Empire romain*, Paris 1958, p.380.
9. Cf. N. Afanassief, 'L'Église qui préside dans l'amour', in *La Primauté de Pierre dans l'Eglise Orthodoxe*, Neuchâtel 1960, p.21; P. Duprey, 'La structure synodale de l'Église dans la théologie orientale', *Proche-Orient Chrétien*, XX, 1970, pp.123–45.
10. Cf. P. Duprey, 'Brèves réflexions sur l'adage "*primus inter pares*"', *La Documentation Catholique* no. 1623, 7 January 1973, p.29.
11. Cf. Ignatius, Romans, introduction; Irenaeus, *Adversus haereses* III, 3, 2.
12. Duprey, 'Brèves réflexions sur l'adage "*primus inter pares*"' (n.10), p.30.
13. Cf. Lateran Council IV (1215), Constitution no. 5; Council of Florence (session VI, 6 July 1439).
14. Cf. the allocution of John Paul II to the Plenary Assembly for the Revision of the Codex of Eastern Canon Law, *Osservatore romano*, 13 November 1988.
15. V. Phidas, '*Primus inter pares*', *Canon* IX, 1989, pp. 184–5.

The Priority of the Preaching of the Word of God, the Liturgy and Diaconia over Doctrine

HANS-JOACHIM SCHULZ

Introduction: creed or dogma?

The pontificate of John Paul II has extended the sphere of church doctrine that is to be regarded as definitive and not open to correction to the secondary interpretation of the tradition, i.e. beyond the doctrinal decisions of the ecumenical councils and the papal *ex cathedra* decisions which were previously regarded as infallible. Thus the *motu proprio*[1] *Ad tuendam fidem* of 18 May 1998, which (accentuating a rescript of 18 September 1989) requires 'the religious obedience of the will and the mind' to the doctrines from tradition which have been inculcated by the pope or the college of bishops in the exercise of their authentic magisterium. From now on, those who assume church office must also explicitly commit themselves to such doctrines in the framework of the *professio fidei* (= confession of faith), following on from the Niceno-Constantinopolitan creed.

The commentary of the Holy Office (= Congregation for the Doctrine of Faith) of 29 June 1998 sees these doctrines in the closest connection with the *divinely revealed* substance of faith; here even the restriction of ordination exclusively to males and Leo XIII's 1906 declaration that Anglican orders are invalid are given as examples of such doctrines, though in liturgical circles the declaration by Leo XIII has long been regarded as untenable.

The incorporation of such traditional doctrines into the *professio fidei* has unhappily undermined this as an act of faith and confession. By comparison with the New Testament confession, which is an act of faith strictly orientated on God's salvation in Jesus Christ, such an obligation seems to be a caricature. The process of the emancipation of confessionalistic church doctrine from the original credal tradition of the church, which in any case has been a long one, here comes to an alarming climax.

In the face of the various manifestations of the disintegration of church doctrine which represent a move out of the context of the real proclamation of the word of God and church life, and above all permeate the history of post-Tridentine theology, it is appropriate to describe briefly here, first, how the apostolic proclamation and the confession as a response of faith originally formed an inner unity and how in the light of the New Testament they are related to liturgy and diaconia. Then we need to ask whether the articulation of the doctrine *of the early church and the councils* is to be related more to the early Christian creed or to be interpreted in the sense of the later concept of dogma, since the liturgy undoubtedly expresses the original confessional and kerygmatic structures in the practice of baptism and the celebration of the eucharist. The Second Vatican Council made it possible in principle to regain the paradigm of a predominantly liturgical articulation of faith by its theology of the liturgy (in the Constitution on the Liturgy) and the way in which it linked up with the tradition of worship in early Christianity and the early church. Moreover – opting for the inner orientation of church doctrine and the possibility of its ecumenical reception – it taught the 'hierarchy of truths' in accordance with their intrinsic connection with the mystery of Christ (Decree on Ecumenism, Art.11) and so at the same time impressively brought to light the inner unity between proclamation, confession and teaching in the context of the diaconal and liturgical life of the church.

I. Apostolic teaching and the life of the primitive community

There is no better indication of the original place of doctrine in the *overall pattern* of church life than in the Acts of the Apostles (2.42). The believers of the primitive community 'persevered in (*proskarterountes*) the teaching of the apostles, fellowship, the breaking of bread and prayer'. Thus the apostolic teaching creates spiritual and emotional space for the believers. It builds up community and makes social action possible (cf. Acts 2.45; 4.32ff.). Its relation to Christ, indeed its origin in the apostles' experience of Jesus, finds realization in the 'breaking of the bread' as the deepest liturgical sign of *koinonia* (= fellowship) and sharing Christ's table. Moreover the teaching is orientated on an echo in prayer, whether in the framework of the Lord's Supper or outside it.

Both preaching, which strengthens *koinonia* within the community, and the proclamation which issues a missionary call to conversion, have the *Christ event* as their origin, centre and goal and are characterized by the specific confession of Christ, the messiah sent by God and raised from the dead. This concentration of the content of proclamatory preaching and teaching is also in principle preserved by Luke's Acts of the Apostles, especially in Peter's sermons in the first chapters (regardless of whether Acts is to be dated to the early 60s or only to the 80s). Paul's own testimony bears witness to his missionary preaching (cf. e.g. I Cor.1.18–24).

The separation of the Christian communities from first-century Judaism did not arise out of a *dogmatic focus* in Christian doctrine. According to the most recent Jewish research, the incorporation of the 'curse against the heretics' into the Eighteen Benedictions of the synagogue (*Birkat ha-minim*) is not an action directed specifically against the Christians.[2] The definitive separation was not brought about by a christology which had become quite intolerable for Judaism (as has often, for example, wrongly been supposed in connection with the Gospel of John). Like the Judaism before it and after it, first-century Judaism above all had a halakhic and not a dogmatic-orthodox stamp. And Christianity, whose missionary activity had of course gone beyond the limits of Judaism, did not need any specific dogmatic and doctrinal statements, for example in the form of the Johannine doctrine of the incarnation. As has only been recognized more recently, the Gospel of John in particular moves in Old Testament traditions and patterns of thought[3] (cf. John 1.1 as a quotation of Gen.1). The confession required by the Gospel of John does not relate, say, to a divine 'nature' of Jesus (in the sense of the Council of Nicaea) or to a 'second person' of God, but completely to the *messiahship* of Jesus (John 20.31).

The New Testament does not have a doctrine of the Trinity (in the sense of three persons or hypostases of God). Matthew 28.19 and various later Pauline passages, later understood strictly in terms of a theology of the Trinity, like I Cor.12.4–6 or II Cor.13. 13, show the way in which confessional forms with a triadic structure came into being. This happened in connection with baptism and the eucharist, and as an expression of the way in which God's redeeming love is revealed through his Son in the Holy Spirit and can be experienced in faith.

After the Didache (the 'Teaching of the Twelve Apostles' from the end of the first century), the creed with a trinitarian or triadic structure finally becomes established. Its framework and relation to events can be read off Eph.4.4–6. The candidate for baptism has come into contact with the Christian community. In the course of conversion this community is experienced as the place of the activity of the Spirit (4.4), and this motivated the reception of baptism. Baptism itself is the decisive turn to Christ, indeed it is incorporation into Christ (4.5), albeit in the orientation of all spiritual life on the one God and Father (4.6). Ephesians 4.46 and also Matt. 28.19 are not the echo of a baptismal formula (such a formula exists only from the end of the fourth century, first of all in the East), but a reflection of the dynamic of salvation which proceeds from God, the Father of Jesus Christ, and is especially actualized in baptism and the eucharist (cf. II Cor.13.13). What apostolic teaching and proclamation is in the life of the primitive community is reflected in particular in statements of faith with a trinitarian structure. This is not indoctrination but the experience of salvation coming upon the community; it does not focus on itself and its spiritual fulfilment, but rather represents an awareness of being called to the discipleship of Christ in the service of fellow men and women.

The apostolic teaching is essentially focussed on awakening of faith. This also applies to its elements of theological reflection. In this context doctrine is never merely the communication of truths which can be objectified: what could be defined as 'accord between the intellect and the substance'. The faith awakened or strengthened by the proclamation of doctrine always involves a *personal* relationship between God and human beings. According to scripture, Abraham is the father of faith. 'Against all hope he believed, full of hope, that he would become the father of many nations' (Rom. 4.18). But above all it is true of faith and the truth of the word of Jesus grasped in faith that 'I am the way and the truth and the life' (John 14.6). As exegetical research has shown, the phrase 'full of grace and truth' (John 1.14) brings into play the way in which God's 'grace and faithfulness' belong together in the Old Testament. So faith is never purely a matter of 'holding to be true', but, as the Reformers rightly insist, a matter of staking one's own existence on God, an act of trust in and love of God.

II. The teaching of the councils: a decision on faith?

If church doctrine is not to become detached from church life as a whole, it must be orientated on a proclamation addressed to persons and a response in faith which takes place in the creed and in liturgical prayer. The way in which in modern Catholicism the doctrinal decisions of councils and popes are regarded as decisive criteria for binding doctrine is the result of progressive misunderstandings which began only long after the time of the seven ecumenical councils of the early church and led to a revaluation and over-valuation of the concept of 'dogma' in the late eighteenth century.

Church fathers like Athanasius and Basil, who were themselves the precursors of the ecumenical councils of the early church, did not see the *christological doctrine* of Nicaea (325) as an official doctrinal decision of the episcopate, far less a decision 'on the faith'.[4] Athanasius in particular never tired of asserting that the fathers of Nicaea simply wanted to testify to the Catholic faith which was there from the beginning. To the Greek fathers, and especially Basil, the word 'dogma' seemed quite inappropriate for describing the faith of the councils. For the Greek word *dogma* denotes a 'semblance of truth' and discretion open to alternative decisions. Therefore while a disciplinary decision like the fixing of the date of Easter at Nicaea can be designated 'dogma', the christology of this council cannot; for the fathers it is the apostolic 'kerygma' which is being expounded and made present here.

In relation to doctrine, the term 'dogma' denotes a doctrinal view which is not binding, above all a heretical view. The prevalence of this meaning of the word can easily be verified from the decisions of the council. The Council of Trent still knows the term dogma above all in the phrase *falsum dogma* (= false dogma), the false teaching of the heretics.

It was only at the time of the Enlightenment and rationalism that for the first time the Bavarian Fransciscan theologian Philipp Neri Chrismann (1751–1810) gave the term dogma the meaning of a definition of faith infallibly presented by the supreme magisterium, drawn from revelation.[5] Chrismann's work was then put on the Index of forbidden books, because he was accused of reducing the faith binding on the church to formal decisions of the magisterium, without evaluating the whole of the material of faith in accordance with tradition, especially the teaching of the church fathers. It was only in the pontificate of Pius IX that people in Rome hit on the voluntaristic-juridical term 'dogma', which the pope now used extensively. One can find it often in this form in the text of the doctrinal decisions of Pius IX.

III. The baptismal creed and the eucharistic prayer as the main paradigms of the church's faith

So if the modern concept of dogma as the paradigm of church teaching is very late and of doubtful origin, today we need to look at the real *paradigms of binding statements of faith* which are accepted in the ecumene. They can be found in the primal situations of community life, always when the liturgical proclamation of the word of God from scripture finds its response in confession and prayer, above all in the context of the celebration of baptism and the eucharist. As I already indicated in the exegesis of Eph. 4.4–6, God's salvation through Jesus Christ in the Holy Spirit finds a dynamic expression in the trinitarian baptismal creeds which are binding on individual Christians and at the same time bring them into the life of the community, permeated by the Spirit. The degree to which the saving event is itself articulated and actualized in the confessions is manifested particularly clearly in the celebration of baptism in the first four centuries. At this time threefold immersion was practised – related to the articles of the creed which were spoken in the form of questions from the baptizer and answers from those being baptized. The most important parts of the so-called Apostles' Creed occur for the first time with this function in the *Apostolic Tradition* of the Roman presbyter Hippolytus at the beginning of the third century. The creed was then gradually extended and constantly recited before additionally being handed on to candidates for baptism in the catechumenate within the Roman liturgy as a summary rule of faith. It was accepted by them as an abiding obligation of faith.

Granted, the Niceno-Constantinopolitan Creed did not grow directly out of the liturgy. But the fathers of the Council of Nicaea had before them various local creeds from the practice of catechesis and baptism in the East, the content of which they formulated in a form directed against the Arian heresy. So they created a text (the 'Horos' of 325) the antithetical phrases and concluding anathemas (formulas for exclusion from the churh community) of which were far removed from liturgical language. This formula was no longer a confession for the communities as the basis of faith, but above all a help to bishops who had to grapple with the Arian heresy in making decisions. As an exposition of christological preaching for the church as a whole, however, the Nicene creed itself is regarded as 'kerygma', i.e. as an obligation of faith which is not imposed by the magisterium of bishops as a specific obligation.

Unlike the historical text of Nicaea, the Niceno-Constantinopolitan Creed (which adopted the decisive teachings of Nicaea) was again formulated as a *potentially liturgical* text at the Council of Constantinople in 381. Although it was not primarily created for that purpose, it was apparently soon brought into the framework of the catechumenate and the celebration of baptism in the city of its origin. After the Council of Chalcedon (451) the creed also became established with this function in other patriarchates in the East, and in times of stronger Byzantine domination in Italy for a while even in Rome. Then the creed came to be used definitively in the liturgy of the Roman rite from the eleventh century on in the festal form of the Roman mass. Since then it has been in binding use there as the 'Constantinopolitan creed'.

In a great improvement on the pure Nicene creed, the Niceno–Constantinopolitan creed renounces antithetical observations and does not focus the doctrine of the Spirit, which was the main issue in 381, in the same way as the christology of the Nicene creed. It is not formally said that the Holy Spirit is 'of one substance' (*homoousios*), but only that he is 'worshipped and glorified with the Father and the Son'. Here we find the pedagogical wisdom of St Basil, whose thought was strongly influenced by salvation history and was related to scripture and the liturgy; he also avoided pointed theological terms where possible.

In Basil it is also evident how a *eucharistic prayer* can be the best theological means of expressing the church's tradition of faith without losing the character of a thanksgiving to God motivated by salvation history. The eucharistic prayer (anaphora) of St Basil, which once was preferred to the anaphora of Chrysostom in the Byzantine form of the Orthodox Church liturgy and which is still used on ten days of the church's year, shows how a liturgical prayer can claim priority over dogmatic texts as a testimony of faith,[6] especially since it has its place in the eucharistic liturgy as the centre of church life and in the course of the celebration responds to the proclamation of the word of God in the reading and the gospel.

The eucharistic prayer of Hippolytus in particular is also marked by quite similar qualities; moreover it is formulated in clear analogy to the questions and answers of faith in baptism, so that in Hippolytus baptism and eucharist clearly emerge as the primal situations of the articulation of the church's faith. The creed-like quality of such texts is also a factor today, in particular by comparison with conciliar and papal doctrinal texts of a dogmatic kind which have been formulated in an authoritarian way and which often do not avoid the danger of divorcing church doctrine from the central processes of church life. The liturgical reform of Vatican II did well to introduce as the first of the three new eucharist prayers a text shaped after the model of Hippolytus' eucharist; in the baptismal liturgy – on the model of the questions at baptism in Hippolytus; at the same time it also restored the creed as a whole in the question-and-answer form which in the post-patristic Western rite of baptism immediately precedes the threefold immersion (or infusion).

IV. 'Hierarchy of truths' – the orientation on proclamation and the realization of faith

As well as attaching new importance to the liturgy as the centre of church life, Vatican II also gave an important impetus to the concentration of doctrine and its consistent integration into the life of the church by formulating the principle of the 'hierarchy of truths'. The formulation of this principle of the *different weighting* of authoritatively taught truths, depending on the degree to which they are connected with the *mystery of Christ* as the foundation of faith, was already welcomed warmly by the observers from the Reformation churches during the council. Would the doctrines governed by controversy and differentiation which had been so strongly emphasized since the Coucil of Trent now retreat behind the fundamentals that the Christian churches had in common?

At the council, and later from the Catholic side, it was of course always emphasized that the 'hierarchy of truths' was not a principle of selection, but only a matter of different weighting, and that none of the teaching ever made dogma by the church was being given up as a result. But could not wider conclusions be drawn from this cautious interpretation, which in the course of the council negotiations over the Decree on Ecumenism was already being influenced by the power of the Curia in the plenary council, as a result of the later shifts in the Constitution on Revelation? As is well known, the council refrained from speaking of the tradition of the church as a 'second source of revelation' alongside scripture.

But if scripture (or better, the apostolic teaching laid down in it), in order to be the sufficient revelation of salvation still in fact only need interpretation from the context of the life of faith in *liturgy* and *diaconia,* stamped by the New Testament; in other words, if it does not need to be supplemented by additional propositional truths from tradition, then one could regard the 'hierarchy of truths' itself as a principle which gives priority to an interpretation related to life of the truth of salvation, a principle which is founded on scripture and is to be grounded from scripture.

In particular, however, no special sphere of 'moral doctrine' is to be demarcated within the 'hierarchy of truths', from which revealed norms of moral theology present in the tradition can be made dogma. Granted, the popes since Pius XI also extend the infallibility of papal *ex cathedra* decisions – postulated by Vatican I for the spheres of the 'doctrine of faith and morals' – to moral and even sexual teachings which are to be ultimately binding, but this is a misunderstanding of the Tridentine decree on tradition. In respect of scripture and tradition, this decree taught that the gospel of Christ is 'the source of all truth of salvation and moral order' (*morum disciplinae*). Here a reference to the baptismal command of Mark 16.15 makes it clear that this is the Christian order of life resulting from the obligation to be baptized, and not *morum disciplina* in the sense of a specific doctrine of morality,[7] or even rules for sexual life.

Unfortunately the reception of the principle of the 'hierarchy of truths' in post-conciliar Catholic theology has not been very innovative. Beginning with the 'dogma of the Trinity', it has often been seen only as a framework for a cataloguing of the traditional dogmas which is to be approached logically, and there has been no reflection on the fact that (as I indicated at the beginning) the trinitarian statements of scripture are utterly rooted in salvation-historical thought and orientated on the liturgy. In connection with the strict interpretation of article 11 of the Decree on Ecumenism it needs to be emphasized time and again that here it is explicitly stated that every doctrine is to be related to the *mystery of Christ*, and this also emerges from the direct reference to Eph. 4 as well as Eph. 3.8, a chapter which is centred on the baptismal event as the making present of the mystery of Christ. Accordingly the 'hierarchy of truths' is not a principle for cataloguing individual objectifiable truths which stand by side but a *principle for making saving truth present* as reality. This principle can of course be linked in a *trinitarian* way to scripture (cf. Eph. 3.3–6), but that does not mean the pre-eminence of any particular conciliar dogmas as such.

As a principle for making salvation present the 'hierarchy of truths' needs quite urgently to be related to the encounter with Christ in baptism and eucharist; above all it focusses reference to individual 'defined dogmas' primarily on fundamental discipleship of Christ in accordance with those criteria which the Lord on his return will use to determine whether or not his teaching and action have been followed (cf. Matt. 25.35–40).

No objections can be made to this interpretation either from the concept of 'hierarchy' or from that of 'truth'. For in its oldest meaning in the history of theology the word 'hierarchy' has only a very derivative connection with the range of church offices and their individual functions. As is already clear from the title of the two main works by Dionysius the Pseudo-Areopagite, one of the most influential church writers in the history of theology, who himself belongs to the fifth century but is influenced by Neoplatonism, here the 'church hierarchy' reflects the 'heavenly hierarchy' through a *progressive process of knowledge and the communication of salvation*. So in the history of theology 'hierarchy' is a term belonging to the dynamic of salvation. Similarly (as I have already remarked), in the light of the New Testament and the Bible 'truth' is a personal concept of the self-communication of God in Jesus Christ and the identification of the hearer of the revelation of Jesus with Jesus himself. Accordingly, in the thought of the councils of the early church too the word 'theo-logy' has primarily to do with the Logos which God himself speaks in the person of Jesus Christ and the kerygma proclaimed as Logos, and very little to do with purely philosophical wisdom and doctrinal opinions (which in the terminology of the councils concerned are dismissively designated 'dogma').

So in the light of patristics and above all the New Testament, the 'hierarchy of truths' is rightly to be understood only as the dynamic process of salvation whose 'truths' reflect and realize the one great truth of the God who reveals himself in Jesus Christ. The focal points of this process in the life of the church are the proclamation of the word of God with the response in prayer and above all the liturgical celebration of baptism and the eucharist. However, both main sacraments – as a commitment to Jesus Christ and a meal shared with him – are at the same time the source and impulse of *discipleship* of Christ. The eucharist as 'doing in memory' says just as much as the *proclamation* of Christ (cf. I Cor.11.26) and also the *discipleship* of Christ (so that when Paul censures people in Corinth for scorning fellowship he believes that the celebration of the Lord's supper in which they are engaged is not a real one: I Cor.11.20ff.).

The derived church processes of expounding and inculcating teaching have also to correspond to the dynamic of salvation sketched out here, which manifests itself especially in the hearing of the word and the liturgy. These, too, do not culminate in a definition of doctrine, even as 'a decision on faith', and cannot in particular circumstances lay claim to 'infallibility'.[8] The Vatican II Constitution on Revelation has made it clear that not even scripture is completely free from error and that *a priori* no central spheres of the 'doctrine of faith and morals' can be extracted from it as also being free from error. Rather, it is God himself who realizes his purpose of salvation through scripture (as it is). Therefore if the papal magisterium postulates a form of recognition and freedom from error for spheres of the 'doctrine of faith and morals' which can be marked out in advance, and which the council did not even allow to scripture (or which could not be based on the essence and aim of scripture), it is being hybristic.

Of course, the councils of the early church also already promulgated clauses which excluded people from the church's communion (anathemas) and used these to back up its doctrinal canons. But the basis for these was not a definitive inerrancy of a highly magisterial decision of faith, of the kind that is inherent in the modern concept of dogma. Rather, teaching was a way to salvation and there was the danger of forfeiting salvation if one followed heresies which the bishops were convinced perverted the Christian kerygma. So in the light of the history of the councils, too, church doctrine cannot primarily be intended as an error-free knowledge in questions of faith; it can only be an exegesis of the apostolic kerygma.

The great ecumenical significance of the Constitution on Revelation and the Decree on Ecumenism with its doctrine of the 'hierarchy of truths' is that it did justice to the authentic concept of faith as dependence on the person of Jesus Christ, the Revealer of the one great truth of the saving purpose of God himself. And in particular the council was far more concerned with the renewal of the liturgy, its central role as the proclamation of the word of God and encounter with Christ, and its impulse to discipleship of Christ and diaconia than the mere inculcation of doctrines from the church's traditions.

Translated by John Bowden

Notes

1. In legal language a *motu proprio* denotes a papal degree which is written in the form of a letter, but without an address, because it is written on the pope's 'own initiative'. Depending on the content and purpose, it is legally effective either as a law or an administrative act. A 'rescript' – comparable to the *motu proprio* – is a legally effective written administrative act which is formulated as an 'answer' to a question.
2. For the relevant results of research cf. e.g. J. A. T. Robinson, *The Priority of John*, London 1985, p.74–81.
3. For a summary see K. Berger, *Theologiegeschichte des Urchristentums*, Tübingen and Basel 1995, p.516, etc.
4. For the self-understanding of the ecumenical councils of the early church see H. J. Sieben, *Die Konzilsidee der Alten Kirche*, Paderborn 1979; H. J. Schulz, *Bekenntnis statt Dogma. Kriterien der Verbindlichkeit kirchlicher Lehre*, Quaestiones Disputatae 163, Freiburg 1966, pp.107–79.
5. W. Kasper, *Dogma unter dem Wort Gottes*, Mainz 1965, 36, etc.; Schulz, *Bekenntnis* (n.4), pp.164–8.
6. For the anaphora of St Basil as the comprehensive and most valuable liturgical testimony of faith in the conciliar period of the early church, cf. ibid., pp.385–93.
7. This was already made clear by J. Beumer, *Die mündliche Überlieferung als Glaubensquelle*, Handbuch der Dogmengeschichte I,4, Freiburg 1962, p.85 etc.
8. The debate over papal 'infallibility' may be regarded as settled theologically since the works of Hans Küng, *Infallible? An Inquiry*, London ²1994, and *Fehlbar? Eine Bilanz*, Zurich 1973.

Patterns of *Koinonia* in the First Christian Centuries

ANGELO DI BERARDINO

I. 'Great church' – communion of saints

Celsus, an external and hostile observer of Christianity, who lived in the second part of the second century, watched the teeming growth of sects with the name Christian which competed with one another in referring to Jesus Christ (in Origen, *Contra Celsum* 5. 61–52). He wrote: 'They hurl the most tremendous insults against one another, many of them unspeakable, and they are not disposed to give an inch in the direction of concord' (5.64). Among the various currents in the competition and conflict, Celsus gives first place to that sect which seems to have the largest number of members and the most doctrinal importance, calling it 'the great church' (5.59). The expression took on, and is still used by historians today, with different meanings, to distinguish the orthodox church from the heretics and groups which are marginal by virtue of their doctrine and behaviour. Christianity – the great church – at the time of Celsus was not monolithic in structure, teaching and liturgy. The differences were sometimes very marked, but became less so with the passing of time: for example, there were differences over the date of the celebration of the festivals of Easter and its theological content, in the spheres of christology, and in numerous disciplinary, liturgical and sacramental norms. Criticizing the combative spirit of Christians, the same Celsus recognized that the element which brought their different communities together was their faith in Christ, so that they distinguished themselves from the Jews and of course from the pagans.

1. The criterion of correct faith

If we now look at these communities of the 'great church' from an internal perspective, we see that they felt bound together by a profound sense of belonging to a single essential and constitutive reality: a strict bond with God which formed and was the basis of the union between all the faithful and between communities. The local church and the universal church are 'us'. The idea of 'communion in the holy', whether by this was meant participation in the 'holy things' (the eucharist) or the 'community of the saints', i.e. the faithful, was based on this. Salvation comes from God as his gift and first of all creates communion with him; this soteriological basis is the foundation of communion both between individual believers in a particular community, presided over by its bishop, and between the communities scattered over the ecumene. The church has its origin and its foundation in God, so that there can also be talk of the pre-existent church: 'It is the Spirit, or the triune God, who is the foundation and origin of all the churches and thus forms the permanent principle of their unity' (H.-J. Sieben, DSp 1751). Cyprian of Carthage (died 258) wrote a work on the unity of the church, which he defined as the 'sacrament of unity' (*De unitate* 4 and 7, *Epistles* 45,1; 69.6; 73.11, etc.). In this connection St Augustine says: 'By means of that which is common to the Father and the Son, they have wanted us to be united among ourselves and with them, and by means of this gift to gather together in unity, mediating the one gift which they have in common, which is the Holy Spirit, God and gift of God' (*Sermon* 71.12,18). This union is also realized on the social level, between the local communities, and on the doctrinal level, in the unity of faith, the sacraments and ecclesial discipline. A literature with a canonical liturgical character arose for the two last aspects, which developed and adapted itself to time and place. The doctrinal criterion also changed in the course of time, moving from broad flexibility to great rigidity. The criterion of correct faith took on increasing importance for ecclesial communion, especially in the trinitarian and christological discussions of the fourth to seventh centuries, and led to the elaboration of a common symbol of faith, as a Christian identity card over against the variety of the heresies. The very term symbol is understood as a sign of recognition among Christians (cf. Rufinus of Aquileia, *Commentary on the Creed* 2); 'It is called symbol because Christians recognize one another in it' (Augustine, *Sermon* 213.2). It was also sometimes written on tablets as an apotropaic sign.

The primitive presentation of heresy was simple and linear: the Father had sent the Son, who preached and founded the church, and Christ then sent the apostles to spread the true faith. Wicked persons, instigated by demons, had introduced the heresies after the apostolic period, which was considered pure and innocent, as Hegesippus already wrote in the second century: 'The church remained a virgin, pure and undefiled; if there were any who were trying to corrupt the sound standard of the preaching of salvation, they were still then lurking, as it were, in some obscure and dark hole. But when the sacred band of the apostles had ended their lives in various ways . . . then godless error began to take its rise, and form itself through the deceit of those who taught another doctrine' (Eusebius, *Church History* 3, 32,7–8).

2. *The initial purity*

The presentation of heresy and the attitude of the heretics expounded by Hegesippus quoted in the passage above and in other reports by Eusebius is repeated almost throughout antiquity; moreover these aspects were successively enriched and amplified: the simplicity and purity of the initial faith, the teaching hidden among the heretics, the deception, their evil conduct. However, we know that historically things were very different and much more complex. In any case the polemic, the persecution, the opposition and the social marginalization forced people to close ranks, or better to encourage a more convinced awareness of their own identity in the numerous liturgical, doctrinal and disciplinary differences in the various local and regional communities. Christian identity was affirmed on various fronts. Moreover in a hostile and suspicious society it was indispensable for Christians to present their true nature and identity with a clarification of their own history, their own doctrine and their own way of life.

The Christians of the first centuries found and practised ways of preserving and promoting communion, unity of faith and discipline among the numerous communities scattered above all within the Roman empire and in the autonomous political units of subsequent centuries. These ways, which were more or less useful and effective, were indispensable because there were many and sometimes marked varieties; moreover the communication and circulation of ideas was very problematical. Nevertheless, the organized forms for ensuring unity developed strongly to the point of sometimes attaining definitive configurations. So I shall examine some of these instruments for promoting ecclesial communion. First, however, it seems important to point out that in the process of securing ecclesiastical peace the laity were increasingly marginalized, whereas in earliest times the role which they played was by no means secondary. For example in the third century the councils were held in a public assembly: the laity, too, travelled with 'letters of communion' so that they would be welcomed in other communities, and the laity too were guardians of the orthodoxy of their bishop. But how could an ordinary believer be certain of his orthodoxy? The answer was simple: if he was personally in communion with his bishop, and that bishop was in turn in communion with other bishops, in particular with the great apostolic sees.

II. Care offered through letters

The usual pattern, which was practised intensely from earliest times, was
to put oneself in contact and remain in contact with the other Christian
communities, especially the earliest and the most important, in order to
verify one's own faith and ecclesial practice. Paul himself went to Jerusalem,
fourteen years after his conversion, taking Barnabas and Titus with him, to
meet the other apostles: 'I laid before them (but privately before those who
were of repute) the gospel which I preach among the Gentiles, lest somehow
I should be running or had run in vain' (Gal. 2.2). The Jerusalem community was aware of this responsibility for the proper spread of the gospel with
a right to intervene in missionary activity. Ignatius of Antioch bore witness
to his awareness of the communities with which he came into contact on
his journey as a prisoner to Rome; he also sent them letters. There was a
frequent exchange of letters between the various communities, so that 'the
church which is in Rome' felt that it was not only united but was a unity with
'the church which is in Corinth'.

In the second century a great many people turned to Rome, some to
disseminate their doctrine there, others to cultivate contacts with the
Roman church and compare teachings: Justin, Tabercius, Tatian, Polycarp,
Montanus, Hegesippus, Irenaeus, Origen, Valentinus, Marcion, Theodore
of Byzantium, Noetus, etc. Irenaeus expressed the idea of comparing teaching with those of other churches when he wrote: 'But since it would take too
long in this work to list the successions in all the churches, let us take the
greatest and earliest church which is known to all, the church founded and
established at Rome by the two most glorious apostles Peter and Paul. It is
necessary for every church, that is the faithful who come from every region,
to be in accord with this church, by virtue of its most excellent origin' (*Adv.
haer.* 3,3,2).[1] Hegesippus from the East first went to Corinth and then to
Rome, where he remained for some years; he wrote the memoirs of his
travels in which he related how 'he associated with very many bishops and
that he had received the same teaching from all' (Eusebius, *Church History* 4,
22, 1).

The frequent contacts between the churches were necessary not only
in order to compare the doctrines received, to reject those which were
erroneous and to strengthen one another in the same faith. Relations were
maintained by Christians travelling from one community to another and by
the exchange of letters. Ecclesiastical communion was not identified with
universal uniformity, but was that of individual churches with the main
churches. Tertullian gives an effective summary: 'The churches, since their

roots are apostolic, numerous and great though they are, are always one and the same original apostolic church from which all have their origin. And all being one, they are all first and apostolic. Then such unity is attested by their communication of the peace and the recognition of one another as sisters and the exchange of tokens of hospitality' (*De praescrip.* 20.8). In the following centuries, too, the official exchange of letters between the bishops, especially of the great sees, continued. Their interventions, for want of one central authority, also included admonition, exhortation and instruction.

III. The development of a common symbol of faith[2]

The numerous very brief doctrinal formulae from the first two centuries were too diverse. The trinitarian formula of Matt. 28.19, connected with the baptismal rite, grew in length and content over the first two centuries. It was presented to the candidate at baptism in the form of questions, as happens today in the renewal of baptismal promises on Easter Eve. At the same time a christological confession developed in professions of faith linked to teaching and preaching, which dealt with the human life of Jesus; perhaps used in the administration of baptism, it too was also adopted for other occasions. At some point, we do not know precisely when, the two formulae were fused in such a way as to produce a synthesis which constituted the nucleus of the Apostles' Creed; this can be found in many Christian writers of the second and third centuries (cf. e.g. Irenaeus, *Adv. haer* 1.10 and 13; 3.4). However, the various formulae, brief thought they were, like the longer ones, differed from community to community. In the course of the second century another type of summary doctrinal formula developed which appears in many writers, but not linked to baptism: it summed up the faith and the teaching of the communities in which it was a testimony. Tertullian (*De praescript.*13) offers a detailed outline of it; the order and content correspond to the Roman creed of the fourth century, but in reality it is the outline of the teaching given to catechumens.

It was given different names: rule of truth, rule of faith, rule of piety, etc. So we have two types of profession of faith: one structured with questions and answers and used at the moment of baptism, and the other taking the form of a declaration. Moreover the usage developed of 'delivering' this second formula during Lent to the catechumen, who had to learn it by heart, and 're-delivering' it publicly before baptism. Basil of Caesarea attests that a written profession of faith was made for baptism: 'As for the profession of faith which we set down on our first entry (to the community) when we put away idols and drew near to the living God, whoever does not guard it on every occasion and adhere to it throughout his life as to a sure safeguard, puts himself outside the promises of God, going against what he wrote with his own hand and set down as a profession of his (own) faith' (*De spiritu sancto* 10, 26). The Latins called this *symbolum*, and a legend arose, which was already widespread in the fourth century, that all the apostles before parting from one another each composed a clause of it. The legend reveals a deeper truth in the belief of the fathers: the symbol of the profession of the faith was the most controllable way of expressing the perfect communion of love of Christ and the same doctrinal view.

Although the doctrinal formula differed in detail from church to church, it also became a proof of the perfect and right faith: in other words it was the *locus* where the brothers met among themselves and with God; at the same time it was an instrument of exclusion. The practice attested in Origen's *Dialogue with Heraclides* where there was any doubt about the correct faith of anyone was a public confrontation in church. A formulation of faith was put to the accused; if it was accepted and confirmed communion, the 'peace' was immediately restored; but if it was rejected, a sharp confrontation began. After the Council of Nicaea in 325, in order to escape any doubt about his orthodoxy, Eusebius sent a profession of faith to his church affirming that it was what he had studied in his training as a catechumen and that it matched the creed developed at Nicaea. The various councils of the fourth century simply developed formulations as a sign of their own doctrinal identity, preoccupied in finding a formula on which all could agree. To a degree, the creed of the council of 381 was established when it was accepted by the Council of Chalcedon in 451: on the one hand it was the instrument of communion, and on the other it also became a reason for conflict with the introduction of the *filioque* in the West.

IV. Ordinations and episcopal assemblies

Episcopal assemblies arose and developed naturally to respond to the needs of the Christian communities from earliest times. The Acts of the Apostles (ch.15) relates a meeting of apostles and Christians from various cities to resolve the very sensitive problem of the conditions for admitting Gentiles to Christianity. The unanimous decision arrived at was communicated to the other Christian communities: 'it seemed good to the Holy Spirit and to us . . .' (Acts 15.28). The practice of holding councils, which always had a regional character, developed slowly, but the first evidence of important assemblies goes back to the second half of the second century in the East. In the Roman province of Asia (the Western part of the Anatolian peninsula) there were assemblies to combat Montanism. Tertullian refers to these when he writes that in the Eastern regions there were meetings of 'councils formed by all the churches which discussed the most important questions together' (*De ieiunio* 13.6). Conciliar activity developed and was better organized in the course of the third century. The emperor Constantine resorted to this practice to resolve the Donatist question (Rome, 313; Arles, 314), and then the Arian and the Easter questions (Nicaea, 325).

1. The great councils

In the fourth century, for doctrinal and disciplinary reasons, conciliar activity came to a climax without resolving the problems under discussion, the solution to which was entrusted to theological discussion and the agreement of the bishops of the most important sees. However, the only way to have a fruitful dialogue seemed to be to hold meetings of bishops. The great councils were all convened and approved by the emperor, who gave legal and civil force to their decisions. Justin regarded the conciliar canons of the first four ecumenical councils as imperial laws (*Novella* 131 of 545). Moreover the Council of Nicaea added that 'twice a year synods shall be held so that all the bishops of the same province, meeting for the same purpose' discuss their common problems. The Council of Chalcedon in 451 confirmed this prescription for dealing with 'many of the affairs of the church which are in need of reform' (Canon 19: Trullan council, canon 8). The Council of Constantinople of 381 adds: 'According to the norms relating to the administration of the diocese it is clear that questions relating to a province must govern the synod of the province according to the directives of Nicaea' (canon 23). Therefore the main aims of the provincial councils were limited, namely to resolve local controversies. Moreover, according to the principle of the territoriality of episcopal authority, bishops had to be prevented from interfering in other communities. Such interference must have happened often, given the abundant conciliar legislation on it.

By participating in councils with a large following of bishops and with an exchange of letters the metropolitan ensured the ecclesial communion of his suffragan dioceses with the other sees. Moreover sometimes the councils produced 'synodical letters' to be sent to other bishops to make known their teaching and disciplinary and liturgical prescriptions. Whereas the provincial and plenary councils, i.e. those of several provinces, ensured a limited communion, the ecumenical councils of the first millennium, all celebrated in the East, guaranteed the communion of the *orbis christianus*, the Christian world. After the Council of Chalcedon in 451, many Eastern Christians (the

Monophysites, the Nestorians and the Armenians) no longer shared in the peace of the church. The successive ecumenical councils all followed the Chalcedonian Definition. Now the Latin participation in these councils was very limited, sometimes reduced solely to the Roman delegation, but the Bishop of Rome took part in them personally.

2. The Latin participation

However, the Latin presence ensured the communion of the Latin West with all the Eastern churches. Through Rome the conciliar definitions and canonical prescriptions of the ecumenical councils were received in the West. It was the Bishop of Rome who was the interlocutor with the Christian East, in that the latter had become aware of the West in relation to an ever more distant East. However, now attention was concentrated between the Old and the New Rome, and the whole of that Christian world apart from the proto-Byzantine empire was ignored; the Eastern Christianities, almost completely ignored, also became autonomous for christological reasons. For them it would prove easier on occasion to establish contacts with the Old Rome.

Episcopal ordinations were important moments for meetings of bishops from the same ecclesiastical province; on such occasions they discussed common problems, preserving and increasing the communion of their communities. The *Apostolic Tradition*, attributed to Hippolytus, at the beginning of the third century prescribes that the election of a new bishop must take place with the participation of the people of the local community: 'The people shall meet on Sunday, in the presence of the college of priests and bishops. These last, with the assent of all, shall lay their hands on the one elected' (ch. 2). The Council of Nicaea (canon 4) lays down that all the bishops of the province should be present, but if this is not possible at least three should take part, having obtained the consent of those absent. Everything had to be confirmed by the metropolitan of the ecclesiastical province, which usually coincided with the civil province. There were significant exceptions: the Bishop of Alexandria had authority over all Egypt, Libya and Cyrenaica; in Numidia there was not a bishop but a primate, the oldest bishop by ordination; in Syria the bishops of several provinces were dependent on the see of Antioch. The Council of Chalcedon specifies the criterion of episcopal ordination: the Bishop of Constantinople ordains all the metropolitans in his sphere of competence, who in their turn confer ordination on the bishops of their own province (canon 28). Episcopal ordination seals and creates a relationship of dependence between churches and therefore a hierarchy of them. Moreover the ordination of persons of other communities and their acceptance in other dioceses without the consent of the candidate's bishop was prohibited. One could write a relevant section of the history of the early church as a history of episcopal ordinations.

V. The care of all the churches

The expansion of Christianity led to the creation and foundation of new communities, creating a deep and vital relationship between the mother churches and daughter churches. Apostolicity was transmitted by means of generation in the faith and thus all the churches were apostolic and catholic. Those churches which preserved a very strong memory of their foundation by an apostle and also as a result of their strategic situation in the Roman political system enjoyed greater authority. Thus there developed the great apostolic sees, which enjoyed mutual esteem and respect. The Council of Nicaea, which did not have the intention of establishing a precise order of graduation, recognized Rome, Alexandria and Antioch (canon 6). Their rank was also recognized in the civil order. The church of Jerusalem was, however, accorded a special honorific role 'according to ancient tradition and custom' (canon 7). The canonical decision was the outcome of former practice, since those churches already exercised a power of government and aid in other communities, some of them far distant. The decision of canon 6 of Nicaea gave place to the theory of the three apostolic Petrine sees: Peter was the founder of the churches of Antioch and Rome, and in his name Mark, called the *discipulus* or even *filius Petri*, founded the church of Alexandria (cf. PL 13,374F-376A; PL 54, 1007). In other words, the preeminence of the three sees arose out of the importance of Peter and thus for apostolic and not political reasons.

1. The origin of the pentarchy

At the Council of Constantinople in 381 the imperial see was also inserted into the Petrine triarchy 'because this city is the new Rome' (canon 3). The council brought the organization up to date in keeping with the new political and ecclesiastical situation. From then on in the hierarchical order of the sees Rome was always put in first place; for the first time the 'pentarchy', which it is specifically called at the Council of Chalcedon, was formed. In this perspective the Bishop of Rome is one of the five patriarchs, indeed the first (cf. Gregory M., *Registr.* II, p.154), but he is the patriarch of the West: *praesidens occidentalis Ecclesiae* (Augustine, *C. Iul* VI, 1, 4, 13; PL 44, 648). Faced with the schism of the Three Chapters, pope Pelagius required the communion of the five patriarchs with superior collegial authority.[3] The institution arose to preserve unity of faith and discipline in essential aspects in a varied ambience. The conviction of the early church assigned a prominent place to the criterion of historical apostolicity as an irrevocable and necessary criterion for ensuring the unity and the ecclesial communion of the one church of Christ. All the churches have to be apostolic, but the mother churches have greater responsibility, also for their organization, for 'being and appearing in a most evident way the three apostolic thrones'.[4] Apostolicity is a historical quality and can also be demonstrated by the lists of bishops of the individual churches. These lists are a chain of transmission of the original and faithful 'deposit' and allow its authenticity to be checked.

The discussion in the preceding paragraph is an introduction to the historical role of mediation and ecclesial unity pursued by the Bishop of Rome from the first centuries on. This role had been changed in the first decades of Christian expansion away from the mother community of Jerusalem.[5] The disappearance of the 'pillars' and the other great missionaries brought with it the danger of the fragmentation of the Christian communities, also because perhaps there were several groups with different tendencies and organizations in the major cities. When the mother church disappeared, the point of reference became the apostles and the places of their mission, in particular Rome, which picked up the heritage of Peter and Paul and also of Jerusalem.[6] Apostolic, political, commercial, economic and social reasons conferred on the church of Rome, the centre of the ecumene, a privileged position and therefore one of encounter and contact between the communities (cf. the greetings in Rom. 16; I Peter 5.13; Col. 4.16). Thus the Roman community occupied a recognized and accepted role in unity and mediation: from as early as the second century on, the churches communicated among themselves by means of the action of Rome (cf. Eusebius, *Church History* 5, 25; 6, 43, 3).

2. The Roman church

The Roman church enjoyed great prestige from the beginnings of Christianity onwards; Paul wrote a letter to it, full of appreciation, since this was not a community which he had founded, and praised its faith 'which is spread throughout the world' (Rom.1.8). I Peter, addressed to the Christians in some provinces in Anatolia, comes from the Roman church. In continuity with it, at the end of the first century I Clement is an authoritative intervention by the Roman community on the occasion of the discord which broke out in Corinth;[7] it puts itself in a climate of solidarity to offer help to a sister church in difficulties. Rome also wrote again to the Corinthians around 170 (Eusebius, *Church History* 4, 23, 11). The reference to the martyrdom of Peter and Paul (ch. 5) and to the apostolic succession as a guarantee of order in the community already heralds the doctrine of the Roman care for all the churches. The prologue of Ignatius' letter to the Romans and the mention of Peter and Paul (ch. 4) bring out its primacy in faith and love. Ignatius also refers to the custom of writing letters from Rome, 'You have taught' (3.1). Irenaeus of Lyons, who has already been quoted, affirms the need to be in harmony with the doctrine of the Roman church; Tertullian (*De praescript.* 32 and 36: 'If you reach Italy you will find there Rome, whose authority also comes to us') and Origen (Eusebius, *Church History* 6, 14, 10) indirectly say the same thing. The Roman *sollicitudo* was also made specific at the level of help. Dionysius of Corinth wrote a letter to the Romans praising their solidarity: 'For this has been your custom from the beginning, to do good in divers ways to all the brethren, and to send supplies to any churches in every city: now relieving the poverty of the needy, now making provision, by the supplies which you have been in the habit of sending from the beginning, for brethren in the mines; and thus as Romans you observe the hereditary custom of Romans, which your blessed bishop Soter has not only maintained, but even advanced, by providing in abundance the help that is distributed for the use of the saints, and by exhorting with blessed words, as a loving father his children, the brethren who come up' (Eusebius, *Church History* 4, 23, 10).

In the following centuries the Roman church considered the guarding of faith and discipline its prerogative (cf. Leo the Great, *Ep.* 115,1). With Pope Damasus (366–384) the Roman see also reinforced its idea of centrality by using the text of Matt.16.18ff.; Pope Siricius (384–99) considered the care of all the churches (II Cor. 11.28) a prerogative of the Roman see.[8] Leo the Great, who vigorously affirmed the primatial role of the apostolic see in the service of the faith of all the churches, respected the decisions of the local synods and the customs and laws of the other bishops, who together with him formed the *collegium caritatis* (*Epp.* 5.2; 6.1; 11.1). The primacy and influence of the Roman church varied from church to church, from region to region and depending on the times. Nevertheless, in antiquity every bishop felt in some way involved in the care of all the churches. If on the one hand this encouraged help and mutual support, on the other it could lead to the overstepping of boundaries and interference in other episcopal sees. The canons of the ecumenical councils on the ecclesiastical circumscriptions were aimed at preserving the competence of each church. The historian Socrates asserts that the decisions of the Council of Constantinople in 381 were taken to avoid interference in other dioceses and other eparchies (groups of several dioceses) (*Church History* V, 8). This piece of information is independent of later theological reflection and arose out of the awareness that the unity of the one church entailed a pure order in collegial government.

Such a role of mediation on the part of Rome between East and West became almost exclusive, since direct contacts between the Eastern and Western churches diminished in late antiquity and the Middle Ages, whether as a result of political separation or as a result of linguistic difficulties. Only Rome in the Middle Ages was in a position to follow this mediation both through the action of a permanent Roman delegate at Constantinople (apocrisarius) from the time of Leo the Great or the presence in Rome of Greek-speaking monastic communities. Various apocrisarii became bishops of Rome and were therefore in a position to know the church of Constantinople. The Eastern churches outside the frontiers of the empire had greater autonomy, with respect to all the patriarchs, and this slowly became a schism after the Council of Chalcedon in 451.

VI. Communion in the liturgy

Ecclesial communion was specifically accepted and professed in the eucharistic prayer by means of the mention of the bishops in the diptychs, which were another instrument of ecclesial communion. These were catalogues of dead or living persons who were commemorated during the liturgical celebration, especially in the eucharistic synaxis. Among other names, the diptychs contained the names of bishops, especially those of the bishops of Rome and the great episcopal sees with which they were in communion. However, the names of those bishops who were excluded from ecclesial communion had to be removed. In times of friction and theological struggle the diptychs were constantly rewritten.

The use of the diptychs was intended to express the communion which existed in the Christian community, even between distant peoples, as Dionysius the Areopagite wrote: 'The most holy embrace is exchanged and there is the mysterious and supernatural recitation of the names written on the tablets. Nor in fact is it possible that those who are divided one from another can meet together before the One and participate in the peaceful union of the One with them' (*Ecc. hier* II, 3,8; PG 3, 437A). For this reason the *nomen in sacris diptycis scriptum* was a sign of sacramental communion with the persons nominated and a judgment on the correctness of their faith (so it was also sometimes called *liber vitae*). Of course it was not possible to include the names of all the living bishops, so only those of the main sees were set down; these were in turn in communion with the bishops of their own province or the other great geographical areas (the pentarchy).

Conclusion

I have several times emphasized the sending of letters: it was the usual way of being in communion with the other churches and in contact with the major episcopal sees.[9] The usage goes back to the experience of diaspora Judaism. It helped Christians to maintain and develop the awareness of being a unity of many communities, as it were a 'federation of churches', in which there was a hierarchy of importance, reference and co-ordination. In the East the sees referred to were those of Alexandria, Antioch in Syria and, from the end of the fourth century, Constantinople. This concentrated increasing attention and gave these sees a kind of primacy by comparison with the other great oriental sees. The presence of the emperor in the capital attracted numerous bishops who, during their stay in the city, could form a kind of permanent council.

The exchange of letters between the centres and the peripheries was customary at Easter, at a time when only a few people were in a position to calculate the date of the celebration precisely. At the Council of Arles in 312, a great Western council, the bishops wrote to Pope Sylvester: 'First of all, as for the observance of the Pasch of the Lord: this is to be observed by us throughout the world on the same day and at the same time; and you, as custom requires, are to send letters to all (on this subject)' (canon 1). It was already a custom for the West; there had to be something similar for the East. At all events, at the Council of Nicaea of 325 it was established that the church of Alexandria would calculate the date of Easter and communicate it to the major churches, who would then make arrangements to inform the other communities with circular letters. In the West the letter was sent only to Rome, which in its turn sent it on to the Latin churches. The annual – festal – letters which the patriarch of Alexandria sent to hundreds of bishops in his area of influence were famous.

On the election of a new archbishop in the patriarchal sees it was by the exchange of epistles or synodical letters that full communion of faith was ensured, with the consequent insertion of the names of those newly elected in the liturgical diptychs. The correspondence between the patriarchal sees from late antiquity to the high Middle Ages shows that there was harmonious and collegial government of the universal church, though a special role was assigned to the Bishop of Rome.

A fixed system of communication was necessary, also because at that time there was no canon law, but only local and regional norms and traditions. The dissemination of conciliar canons, including those of the ecumenical councils, was quite limited and the canons were not well known. There was as yet no well defined and equal biblical canon. The Bible, the foundation of Christianity, was the constant point of reference in the life of the Christian communities, particularly in antiquity. Biblical exegesis was the basis of preaching, catechesis, the development of doctrine, of ethics, of institutions and of liturgy and also of controversies. It was a source of unity but also of divisions as a result of the different possible interpretations, depending on the different theologians. Therefore it was meeting and communication, and not the imposition of the old, that really created communion between the churches.

Translated by John Bowden

Notes

1. For this text see especially M. Maccarone, *Apostolicità, episcopato e primato di Pietro*, Rome 1976, pp.42–63.
2. J. N. D. Kelly, *Early Christian Creeds*, London [3]1972.
3. V. Peri, 'La pentarchia: istituzione ecclesiale (IV–VII sec.) e teoria canonica teologia', in *Bisanzio, Roma e l'Italia nell'Alto Medioevo*, Settimane di Studio di Spoleto 34, Spoleto 1988, pp.209–311.
4. Ibid., p.225.
5. H. Hauser, *Église à l'age apostolique*, Paris 1996, p.66.
6. L. Goppelt, *L'età apostolica e subapostolica*, Brescia 1986, pp.173–4.
7. The letter was still read in public in Corinth around 170 (Eusebius, *Church History* 4, 23, 11).
8. L. Padovese, 'Roma e la sollecitudine delle Chiese. Espressione di comunione ecclesiale nei primi tre secoli', in L. Pani Ermini and P. Siniscalco (eds), *La comunità cristiana di Roma*, Vatican City 2000, pp.65–82.
9. Cf. the numerous letters from Dionysius of Corinth, Eusebius, *Church History* 4, 23.

II. Practical Perspectives

'Hierarchy of Truths' – and Ecumenical Praxis

OTTO HERMANN PESCH

The results of ecumenical dialogue, above all dialogue at a high official church level like the 'Joint Declaration on the Doctrine of Justification' (1999), have a realistic chance of being received by 'church people' only if virtually nothing changes for everyday religious life in church and society. This is the experience of all pastors who are active ecumenically. People like to work together where that is possible and where ecumenically committed pastors and church members point the way. Joint educational courses are arranged (lecturers, Bible studies and the like). Ecumenical services are held on notable dates, for example during the Week of Prayer for Christian Unity (18–25 January). But everyday church life – worship, preaching, receiving the sacraments, personal piety – takes place in one's own church. It is only there that personal faith has its 'home', and only there do its specific forms of expression develop.[1]

So while ecumenical bodies may note convergences and pioneer ways to new church unity as far as they want to and can do, the local communities will not accept any form of church unity which results in a *uniformity* of church life and, as its basis, a *unitary* church order. An 'ecumenical church order' can have as its immediate goal only the mutual recognition of the churches *as they are*; anything else is an illusion. Any 'ecumenism of a return to the fold' (to put it from a Catholic perspective) – a Roman Catholic expectation which is suppressed only with some difficulty[2] – and any 'ecumenical connection' – a theological hope of the Reformation churches which is sometimes openly conceded[3] – is thus excluded by the believing common sense of the Christian 'people'. Of course, that does not mean that everything will remain as it is in the churches which recognize one another as the church of Jesus Christ – 'in the proper sense!'. Even ordinary believers who do not want to give up their home in their church for the sake of ecumenism are ready to learn from sister churches: they expect an enrichment of their own piety from getting to know the other traditions. Anything more must be left to historical development. Thank God, not everything can be planned in advance for the future, and to this degree cannot be an element of *present-day* ecumenical 'strategy'.

As I have remarked, that is the result of a sober, perhaps a sobering, look at the reality of the ecumenical movement – but the professionals in ecumenical dialogue have never had to learn it. Now what in fact happens is not in itself a criterion of the truth. So we have to ask: is a recognition of the ecumenical reality theologically sound? It would be sound only if the questions of structure and mentality which stand in the way of a new church fellowship in fact had less weight than the common experience of faith among Christians in the separated churches, in other words, if for *theological* reasons the different forms of life in the churches which cannot *in fact* be made uniform – from church order, through the shaping of the ministries, to custom – need not, indeed may not, be made uniform. This question brings us to the much discussed term 'hierarchy of truths' (*hierarchia veritatum*), which the Vatican II Decree on Ecumenism, *Unitatis redintegratio* (UR), requires ecumenical dialogue to observe (art.11). What does it mean theologically and therefore also practically?

I. A 'ruse of the Holy Spirit'

After a warning against false 'irenecism', the admonition to express Catholic belief 'more profoundly and precisely' in a way which 'our separated brethren' can also understand – the Council thus does not think that these two are always adequate! – and the demand for love and humility in the common search, these sentences follow: 'When comparing doctrines with one another, they should remember that in Catholic doctrine there exists an order or "hierarchy" of truths (. . . *existere ordinem seu "hierarchiam" veritatum*), since they vary in their relation to the foundation of the Christian faith. Thus the way will be opened whereby this kind of fraternal rivalry will incite all to a deeper realization and a clearer expression of the unfathomable riches of Christ.'[4]

These sentences follow word for word a proposal for expanding the Decree made by Cardinal König of Vienna, which was introduced only on 5 October 1964 at the individual voting on the revised text of the decree. It was incorporated by the Secretariat for Unity and accepted by the Council on 11 November at the final vote on the second chapter.[5] The phrase 'hierarchy of truths' is hardly explained, and therefore it immediately provoked a small library of interpretations.[6] Simply from the wording, anyone who reads the two sentences without knowing how the text came into being must come to the following conclusions. 'Hierarchy' means a holy order of precedence. Here it exists between 'truths' (plural), i.e. individual true statements. These stand in a 'holy', i.e. unassailable order of importance and significance for faith and Christian life. The criterion for putting them in this order is the different ways in which they are connected with the foundation of Christian faith. That is to be applied to ecumenical dialogue. 'Thus' – i.e. in such an application – a way will be prepared for 'fraternal rivalry', for 'deeper realization' and 'a clearer expression of the unfathomable riches of Christ'. This statement alludes to Eph. 3.8 and indicates that these features have not so far been sufficiently present – see above – at any rate in the Catholic church.

If words mean anything at all, 'deeper realization' on the basis of observing the 'holy order of precedence' of propositional truths can only mean that agreement with and common confession of *each* of these truths expressed in propositional form cannot be of *equal* importance for the unity of the church. To put it even more clearly: the condition for church communion cannot be that both sides, enumerating schematically the doctrines which divide them, have to arrive at a consensus on *all* these doctrines. A formally equal assent to the faith has to give way before the different meaning of the content; it has to be differentiated in accord with the narrower or wider connection with the 'foundation' of faith.

Now it is possible to discuss what cannot be changed and cannot be given up even for the sake of church communion and what can. The text leaves this completely open: it does not expect a 'rivalry' of understanding – and thus does not exclude the possibility that excessively strict conditions for church unity can, may, indeed must also be reduced. But the complete openness is evident only if we look back at the prehistory of the formulation. This was initially concealed by the last-minute intervention of Cardinal König, but now we have far more information about it. Here again – as in other cases![7] – it becomes evident that the Holy Spirit evidently also reckoned with human bigotry at the Council.

The phrase in fact underwent a development between its first suggestion and the expansion of the final text; in this development its original sense was virtually turned upside down. To be brief,[8] as early as summer 1963, i.e. between the first and second sessions of the Council, the titular bishop of Eleuterno, S. Ferraz, proposed that different phases should be distinguished for the process of a new unity with Protestant Christians. In his view, in a first step it would be necessary to concentrate on the priority of some 'fundamental aspects' of Catholic dogmatics, above all belief in Christ. The other dogmas could easily be 'erected' on this 'fundamental dogma' and made acceptable to the separated brethren. The second step could then be sacramental fellowship and the third and final step 'juridical and disciplinary union'. Here the presupposition was that 'we distinguish between a simple and truly adequate faith and the further deeper understanding of this faith to be attained progressively later, *as also happens among Catholics'*.[9] The request by this (otherwise little known[10]) titular bishop that there should be a concentration on fundamental fellowship in faith in Christ when the conditions for church unity were being discussed is more than ever true today. But as a matter of course the council fathers had as a distant goal an 'ecumenism of a return' of the 'separated brethren' to a 'juridical and disciplinary unity' of the church. The way to this was said to be comparable to the progress from simple to deeper belief among Catholics. So are the 'separated brethren', like young people, on the way to the maturity of an adult faith?[11]

The Dominican C.-J. Dumont, editor of the ecumenical journal *Istina*, took up Mgr Ferraz's proposal in a synthesis of written comments on the forthcoming Decree on Ecumenism. He was likewise working on this decree in summer 1963, on behalf of some bishops. Dumont made a more extensive statement than Ferraz. For the first time we have the literal use of the term 'objective hierarchy' in the articles of faith revealed by God and set before the church, even if they are all as it were to be confessed with firm approval. But as with Ferraz, the 'objective hierarchy' relates to the three stages of the way to 'perfect unity' in the 'fellowship of canonical unity'.[12]

Dumont's proposal for expansion did not find assent in the version laid before the Council. But during the first discussion of the scheme on ecumenism the Italian archbishop Andrea Pangrazio of Gorizia made a speech on 25 November 1963 which cannot be praised highly enough. It brought the turning point and if there were sufficient space, I would love to quote it all.[13] The key points are:

1. The 'quantitative', 'accumulated' enumeration of the fullness of the institutional means of salvation is not sufficient to emphasize the relationship between the Catholic Church and separated Christians; it is important to emphasize the 'bond' and the 'centre' in which they are united. 'This bond and centre is Christ himself, whom all Christians acknowledge as the Lord of the church, whom the Christians of all communities beyond doubt want to serve with a believing heart, and who in

his grace through his active presence in the Holy Spirit achieves such wonderful things even among the separated communities . . .'

2. This bond and this centre – in Ferraz and Dumont the 'foundation' – is not the occasion for a first step to unity which still has to be taken or reflected on; as Pangrazio twice explicitly remarks, it is the basis for a unity of Christians *which already exists.*

3. In order *not only to enumerate but also to weigh up* what the Christian churches have in common and where they differ Pangrazio refers back to Dumont's phrase *hierarchia veritatum.*

4. At the same time he indicates a criterion for weighting: 'There are truths which belong to the *order of the goal,* like the mystery of the most Holy Trinity, the incarnation of the word and redemption, divine love and grace towards sinful humankind, eternal life in the consummation of the kingdom of God, etc. But there are other truths which belong to the *order of the means of salvation,* like the truth that there are seven sacraments, the hierarchical structure of the church [!], the apostolic succession [!], etc.

5. 'These truths relate to the means which are given to the church by Christ *for its earthly pilgrim way; but after that they cease*' (my italics).

It is clear that an objective-theological interpretation has replaced the so-called psychological-pedagogical interpretation of the *hierarchia veritatum* which the 'separated brethren' could only have rejected with indignation – this provides a link to what is said in the Constitution on the Church, *Lumen Gentium* (LG) 15. Here we have the 'ruse of the Holy Spirit'. The distinction between the 'order of the goal' and the 'order of the means' did not find its way into the final text – according to good tradition a council does not interpret itself. In his proposal Cardinal König took up only the key phrase 'hierarchy of truths', and indicated the direction of the interpretation by an open reference to the (objective!) 'connection with the foundation of faith'. But the theological discussion of the council text followed the line of Andrea Pangrazio's approach.

II. The discussion is opened – and open

Thus the decisive unity in faith through the work of the Holy Spirit extends beyond the earthly way of the church, whereas the differences over the 'means' stand with these under the eschatological proviso that one day they will disappear, in accord with LG 48, section 3. There must then already be strong reasons if what in any case is destined to disappear may separate Christianity which exists in a fundamental fellowship of faith. Archbishop

Pangrazio had the courage to mention as examples of such truths about the means which are subordinate to the order of the goal precisely those which are also most controversial in ecumenical dialogue: the sacraments, the hierarchical structure of the church, and the apostolic succession. Nothing of what has developed here in the Catholic Church must be given up, provided that it is not a corruption contrary to the gospel. But before these differences are allowed to split Christianity into mutually exclusive 'fellowships' (as Pangrazio was still saying correctly in 1963), it must be asked to the last possibilities of theology whether and how far the 'means' cannot legitimately be different. To keep to the three examples: how far can the *number* of the church ministries named by the historically contingent name 'sacrament' be divisive if the *understanding* of the relevant ministries is shared, in other words if all that is contained in them is also celebrated, known and lived out in the sister churches, and the differences in any case remain within the normative biblical testimony? How far is the hierarchical constitution of the church, i.e. the specific basic structure of its common life (*koinonia*), including the Petrine office of the Roman bishop, as open to historical change today as it was has been through history? How far may a succession produced by the episcopal laying on of hands – which in any case cannot be historically guaranteed – be made the condition for church fellowship if on the one hand by virtue of the common faith apostolic succession is recognized *in doctrine* and on the other in non-Catholic churches, too, an office of leadership of the church extending beyond the communities is understood as essential for the church?[14] Basically something could be inalienable and not open to discussion in the sphere of 'means' only if it were *directly* connected with the 'foundation of faith' – so that it would itself be abandoned if these means were renounced – in other words, if the activity of the Holy Spirit no longer had a starting point without these means. Who would want to make such a statement about any of the means mentioned?[15] They are all only concrete, i.e. secondary alterations to the primary institutional means without which the church would not be the church. Here the whole history of ecclesiology can be summed up in the list in Acts 2. 42, namely: preaching and teaching (*martyria*), worship of God (*leiturgia*) and community life (*koinonia*), and service to one another and the word (*diakonia*).[16] Thus if Archbishop Pangrazio is right, the ecumenical discussion is open to many possibilities which in dialogue are restricted only by laziness of the spirit and the human heart. And the same goes for ecumenical praxis.

III. Criteria for ecumenical praxis

The reader might now expect a catalogue of proposals for ecumenical praxis in the light of the hierarchy of truths. That is not possible in this short article – simply because of the very different situations in the different regions of world Christianity. Similarly, I shall leave out the whole sphere of joint diaconia, because it does not in any way link up with the question of the hierarchy of truths. Here it is necessary only to appeal to the ecumenical imagination and to readiness for commitment at every level of church life, to be aware of and to realize the countless still-unused possibilities of ecumenical involvement, and in this way to make it possible practically to experience 'the foundation of faith', the 'already existing' unity of Christianity.

Here, taking up the reflections in the first part of this issue, with reference to some controversial situations, I can only indicate that the phrase *hierarchia veritatum* as formulated by the Council under the influence of the 'ruse of the Holy Spirit' can so to speak open up theology if it is taken to heart.

For about two decades the ecumenical process has been dominated by the term 'confessional identity'. This also blocked the lively discussion leading up to the 'Joint Declaration on the Doctrine of Justification'.[17] 'Confessional identity' denotes the whole of theological doctrines, church practice, forms of piety and cultural life which by their reciprocal influence mark out one confessional church from its sister churches and make it possible to term a form of behaviour, a way of thinking, a style of speaking for example 'typically Protestant', 'typically Catholic', etc. Anyone who goes to a Catholic, an Orthodox, a Lutheran, a Reformed (Presbyterian) and a Free Church service one after the other will know what 'confessional identity' is. Originally – i.e. at the beginning of the split! – such confessional identity was bound up with a claim to express the 'only true Christianity', the 'fullness of Christian faith', the 'apostolic tradition'. The dynamic towards 'confessional churches' which followed on the one hand for a long time made the separation impossible to heal, and on the other led to practical and theological forms of Christian faith in which the other churches today – at last – are recognizing a spiritual wealth which they have either lost or of which they have previously been deprived.

Now almost always such confessional identity belongs in the sphere of (truths about the) 'means' and even there only to truths in the sphere of the secondary institutionality of the church in which its primary institutionality, namely witness, worship, fellowship, service, is made concrete. In the light of the hierarchy of truths nothing of such identity need be sacrificed for the unity of Christianity – even a future institutional unity. Indeed nothing *may* be sacrificed, because this would turn spiritual wealth into poverty. And conversely, no one personally, and no church, needs to take over everything that is perceived and indeed recognized as 'typical' of a sister church. The only aspect which has to be put in question and overcome is that of marks of identity which once were developed or maintained exclusively for purposes of separation, for example the reservations against communion in two kinds which are still maintained in the Catholic Church, of the Protestant reservations about more 'sensual enjoyment' and liturgical festivity in worship.

It is easy to guess what a liberating effect the hierarchy of truths would have on the sore points of confessional identity if it were taken seriously. To add to the examples mentioned by Archbishop Pangrazio (see above): can reciprocal admission to the Lord's Supper still be refused for *theological* reasons – pastoral, psychological and church-political objections are another matter – where after all the Lord's Supper as a whole, independently of its interpretation and practice, belongs to the 'means'?[18] Can a veneration of the saints, purged of all latent superstition, especially the Catholic and Orthodox veneration of Mary, still separate the churches?[19] And if specific church structures which have grown up in history and indeed are time-conditioned were to divide the church, would that not imply that the church itself was on the same level as the goal, and no longer on the level of the 'sign and instrument' (LG 1)? For an 'ecumenical structure of the churches' it follows from this that the legal regulations of community life need to be shaped or reshaped in all the churches in such a way that their function as a *means* for furthering faith in God in Christ is not only affirmed in a theoretical and theological way but also remains evident from outside, also for non-Christians – as an example and not least by virtue of the content and style of official statements.

If that is the case, then the question of ministry and the understanding of ministry which time and again is brought into the foreground is largely reduced to the question of name. The Roman Catholic and the Orthodox churches' emphasis on the ecumenical importance of an understanding of the ministry certainly does not arise out of a need for prestige on the part of those who hold office. On the contrary, they usually understand themselves to be 'useless servants' of Jesus Christ (Luke 17.10). Nevertheless, what can an 'episcopal structure' as a criterion for being a 'proper' church (*Dominus Jesus* 17) seriously mean? If that were the case, for a long time the Roman church would not have been a 'proper church': in the East this episcopate was already a fixed institution, whereas Rome was still led by a presbyterate.[20] For historical and substantive reasons it can only be that outside the office of the local ministry of the preacher and pastor (or a ministry related to particular groups of person) the church has the office of a church leadership which extends beyond the community and in some cases beyond the region entrusted with the task of visitation and ordination – in order to represent the catholicity of the church. Anything else, all legal regulations about the extent and content of the power exercised by those holding a particular office, has always been open in history – and also been the object of power struggles; that may therefore also be the case today, for all this is far removed from the 'foundation of faith' which all offices have to serve as well as they can. But above all, what the minister – male or female – is called is an open question. To be provocative: it is unimportant whether he bears the title bishop, superintendent, patriarch or church president – indeed even whether the office is exercised by an individual or by a body. The office of leadership extending beyond the community is thought to be essential in all the great churches, and even the so-called Free Churches initially had offices extending beyond the community. For the reasons already indicated above, the 'sacramental nature' of ordination is no real problem, and contrary to the views of some it is not understood in a 'semi-magical way' even in the Catholic and Orthodox churches. So there is a wide field for overcoming blockages in understanding in the light of the *hierarchia veritatum*.[21]

IV. A provisional 'church fellowship'

It is therefore time, at the beginning of the new century, to take up again and develop a proposal which Lukas Vischer, at that time General Secretary of the Faith and Order Commission of the World Council of Churches, made in 1974 on the tenth anniversary of the proclamation of the Decree on Ecumenism: the churches should agree on a 'provisional unity' – otherwise the ecumenical movement would 'disintegrate'. Some would return into the old confessional clarity, and the others set off into the no man's land of a 'third confession' with no future.[22] A 'provisional unity' – or better, to dispel any fear of uniformity, a 'provisional church fellowship' – would at the same time have to be more and less than the World Council of Churches. Less, because in the short term it seems inconceivable that some 'small' churches and 'church fellowships' which are now members of the World Council of Churches and should remain so would join this 'provisional church fellowship'. More, because this church fellowship would not be a *council* of churches but a fellowship of churches, which remain these churches, provisionally united as *one* church. This provisionally united church as such expresses the whole of Christianity as living on the 'foundation of Christian faith', related as a historical concrete phenomenon to the

'order of the goal'. All the differences would then be *internal* differences, so
to speak the object of family disputes over the open decisions about the
'means to the end'. Nothing would prevent individual member churches
within this *provisional* fellowship for good reasons from entering into *full*
church fellowship with one another: for example the Orthodox churches
with one another; the Lutheran churches with the Reformed churches, with
the Methodists, with the Anglicans, and these in turn with the Old
Catholics, as indeed has in part already happened in Europe and the USA;
and in the end, hopefully soon in this century, also the Orthodox Churches
with the Church of Rome. At what point *full* church fellowship of *all* provisionally united churches with one another and with those which were still
not united was to take place would have to be left to history, in the certainty
that in this respect too the Holy Spirit brings about 'such wonderful things'
(Pangrazio). If there were no kind of such 'provisional church fellowship', it
could happen that at the end of this century Christianity still existed in two
forms: on the one hand in the form of some great sects and many small sects
in the context of a vast religious pluralism which relativized everything,
and on the other as a 'cultural legacy' of the Western world like Greek
philosophy and Roman law. That would then be the result of human resistance to the Holy Spirit. As a result, while the Holy Spirit would not be
absent from Christianity, it would have to do considerably more to bring
about 'wonderful things'.

We cannot overlook the fact that various churches will have greater difficulties than others over entering into such a provisional church fellowship.
The Orthodox churches of the East with their strong, indeed unbending,
allegiance to the tradition of the first Christian millennium will find it
difficult to relativize in the light of the *hierarchia veritatum* the traditions in
doctrine and church life formed in this period. Conversely, many Free
Churches will view any universal church structure with mistrust, because
they have not forgotten the bitter experiences with the great churches which
were the reason why they split off. Paradoxically, the Roman Catholic
Church could find it easiest, provided that it really received Vatican II in its
doctrine and life. It could learn from the experience of the Orthodox
churches, which are so faithful to tradition, with the synodical principle,
how to break with its centralism, which historically is very late, and which
certainly does not need from the first to the last canon of CIC to be regarded
as 'divine law'. And through its wealth of communities, associations,
brotherhoods, works, orders, sodalities and conferences it has open spaces
where even the most demanding of the Free Churches could find a home: a
meeting together of people who 'in this way want seriously to be Christians'

(Martin Luther) and who expect more from the churches than religious service.

Conclusion: What is to be done?

But what can the Christian in the community, the 'ordinary man' and the 'ordinary woman', now do to live ecumenically in the light of the hierarchy of truths? Here, of course, the different cultural contexts, for which no universal rules can be made, come into play. The ecumenical situation differs depending on whether a community is in a country the overwhelming majority of which is Catholic (as in Spain) or Protestant (as in Scandinavia) or Orthodox (as in Greece), or is completely split confessionally (as in the USA), or where both churches are roughly equal in strength (as in Germany). The situation differs again where Protestant Christians find (found!) the Catholic Church in a pact with the powerful, who want to restrict the scope of their possibilities for development (as in Chile), where Catholic Christians predominantly experience 'Protestantism' in the form of North American communities which – a frequent charge that needs to be examined in detail – offer no resistance to being exploited by economic interests to keep the masses quiet (as in Brazil), or where the Catholic Church (at least many theologians and orders) stands harmoniously with the Protestant Christians on the side of the poor (again as in Brazil and Argentina). The ecumenical situation differs yet again where Christians of all confessions have to live with sometimes militant Muslims (as for example in many places in Africa, in Indonesia and also in Palestine), or where they are regarded as a Western import in a context stamped by Buddhism and in addition even come under suspicion of syncretism in distant Rome if they make serious efforts towards inculturation (as, say, in India or Japan). Generally it will be the case that the more the minority situation is an everyday reality, possibly involving persecution, the more the highly existential understanding of the *hierarchia veritatum* must grow.

For Western cultural circles – and not least for my own country, Germany – it may be said that a Christian with a conscious concern for ecumenism may with a good conscience do what conscientious ecumenical theology has shown to be legitimate. However, Christians must be clear that the churches as a whole, and those who hold office in them, not only may but indeed must be more hesitant because they themselves, or at least many of the people entrusted to them, cannot reflect on the consequences of the hierarchy of truths with equal intensity, and indeed are personally not at all affected by the problems. In that case they will of course initially be more anxious, and those who hold office will often even have to take precautions which they do not need for themselves. They must be primarily concerned that the unity of the church does not collapse – even if that cannot mean that they always wait for the last vehicle in the ecumenical bandwagon. Therefore Christians living with an ecumenical awareness will also take seriously any restraining official statement on ecumenical questions – as most recently *Dominus Jesus* – as an indication of questions which are not yet settled, but need not regard them as the last word on the matter. They must not be deterred from regarding the separated churches as 'sister churches'. They must regard those who hold office in them as holding office in the church – how are they to carry on an honest conversation with them on an equal footing and at the same time objectively regard them as being guilty of arrogating office? They may recognize in other churches things which perhaps are alien to them – and openly expect sisters and brothers from the other church to accept what is distinctive to them, without forcing it on them. They may and should pray with them and worship with them, which for a long time has not been a matter of course for Catholic Christians. With an informed conscience they may also approach the Lord's table in a sister church. For what is conceded for Catholics according to the Ecumenical Directory no.159f. for the marriage of a couple of different confessions and their friends and relations can no longer be regarded as a quite inadmissible exception in other pastoral situations of equal 'existential density'.

Is there a danger of indifferentism? This cannot be ruled out, above all if exceptions which are also experienced as such become custom as a result of repetition, and if, contrary to all good theological and pastoral reasons, the church's officials maintain the grey area of illegality in which the praxis of this so-called *communicatio in sacris* (sacramental fellowship in worship) has long found itself in the confessionally strongly mixed regions of the world church. But there is a good test which conscientious individuals can apply to themselves: the stubborn effort to understand the problems of ecumenism better and better through appropriate reading and education.

The 'provisional church fellowship' would have attained its best inter-mediate goal if a conversion from one church to another – which the Decree on Ecumenism rightly took care to distinguish from ecumenism (UR 4.4) – was no longer regarded as treachery and apostasy, but was respected in the same way as a move from one community to another; in which the person changing finds the home that faith needs in a better, personally more appropriate way.

Translated by John Bowden

Notes

1. Cf. Otto Hermann Pesch, 'Rezeption ökumenischer Dialogergebnisse. Ungeschützte, aber plausible Vermutungen zu ihren Schwierigkeiten', *Ökumenische Rundschau* 42, 1993, pp.407–18; Sabine Pemsel-Mayer, *Rezeption – Schwierigkeiten und Chancen. Eine Untersuchung zur Aufnahme und Umsetzung ökumenischer Konsensdokumente in den Ortskirchen*, Würzburg 1993.

2. What other idea of new church fellowship is left if in the Declaration by the Congregation of Faith, *Dominus Jesus*, No. 17, only the Eastern Churches are accorded the tile of 'true particular churches', and even that with a qualification because they dispute the papal primacy, while all others are described as 'communities' but 'not proper churches'? What would a church in an inauthentic sense be? Not, at any rate the 'church of Jesus Christ' and thus not a church at all – so that the only way to be a church is to return to the Catholic church or an Orthodox church.

3. Cf. Jörg Baur, *Einig in Sachen Rechtfertigung?*, Tübingen 1989, p.27: 'This breach could be healed only if the present-day Roman Catholic Christianity had the experience of the Reformation, and then also clearly said farewell to the Tridentine No.' The same hope has been heard in the vigorous discussion over the Joint Declaration on Justification, no.18, when some Protestant critics have insisted that everything has already been said when the doctrine of justification is the sole criterion of the church. I cannot and must not go into detail on this here.

4. UR 11, last paragraph.

5. Cf. the commentary by Johannes Feiner in *Lexikon für Theologie und Kirche* (*LThK*² 2), *Ergänzungsband* II, Freiburg im Breisgau 1967, pp.88–90; Otto Hermann Pesch, *Das Zweite Vatikanische Konzil. Vorgeschichte – Verlauf – Ergebnisse – Nachgeschichte*, Würzburg ⁴1997, pp.224f.: 232–5; Mauro Velati, *Una difficile transizione. Il cattolicismo tra unionismo ed ecumenismo (1952–1964)*, Bologna 1996, pp.462–4.

6. For a selection see Feiner (n.5); Heribert Mühlen, 'Die Lehre des Vaticanum II über die "Hierarchia veritatum" und ihre Bedeutung für den ökumenischen Dialog', *Theologie und Glaube* 56, 1966, pp.303–35; Uffich Valeske, *Hierarchia veritatum*, Munich 1968 (especially pp.45–67 with the report on the discussion immediately after the Council); Piet Schoonenberg, 'Hierarchia veritatum', *Tijdschrift voor Theologie* 8, 1968, pp.293–8; W. Hryniewicz, 'La hiérarchie des vérités', *Irenikon* 51, 1978, 470–91; Gustave Thils. '"Hierarchia veritatum" (Décret sur l'oecuménisme, n.11)', *Revue théologique de Louvain* 10, 1979; Yves Congar, *Diversity and Communion*, London 1984; Otto Hermann Pesch and Heinrich Fries, *Streiten für die eine Kirche*, Munich 1987, pp.30–5 (Fries); pp.171–6 (Pesch); Armin Kreiner, '"*Hierarchia veritatum*". Deutungsmöglichkeiten und ökumenische Relevanz', *Catholica* (Münster) 46, 1992, pp.1–30. There is some instructive information in Wolfgang Beinert, '*Hierarchia veritatum*', in *Lexikon für Theologie und Kirche*³ (*LThK*³), Vol.5, Freiburg im Breisgau

1996, p.84; see also the various articles relating to the question by Karl Rahner in *Theological Investigations*, Vols 13 onwards.

7. The most significant are the placing of the chapter on 'the people of God' before that on the hierarchical constitution of the church in the Constitution on the Church and the extension of the almost failed declaration on the relationship of the church to the Jews to the Declaration on the Non-Christian Religions. Cf. Pesch (n.5), pp.146–8, 294–303.

8. Details in Velati (n.5), pp.462–4. Here there is also a documentation of the different proposals for the text.

9. *Acta Synodalia Sacrosancti Concilii oecumenici Vaticani II* (AS), II/5, Typis polyglottis Vaticanis 1973, p.891 (my italics).

10. He is not listed in the index of persons in supplementary volume III to *LThK²*.

11. One is reminded of the distinction between the *minores* and the *maiores in fide* in Thomas Aquinas, *Summa Theologiae* II–II 2, 6–8. All must believe some fundamental truths of faith: the *maiores* must examine everything – and be at the disposal of the *minores* if these have questions.

12. Cf. C.-J. Dumont, 'Observations reçues sur le Schema "de Oecumenismo" in genere'. Text in Velati (n.5), p.463 n. 30. Thils, ibid. (n.6), pp.210f., refers to a discussion which had then been going on for twenty-five years and mentions the names of Yves Congar, Karl Rahner, Michael Schmaus and Dumont. There is a report on this in Valeske (n. 6), pp.29–45.

13. Full text in *AS* II/6, 1973, *Congregationes generales* 74–79, sessio publica 3, pp.32–5. There are quotations of the decisive sentences in *LThK²* Supplementary volume 2, pp.88–90, nn.44,49; Pesch (see n.5), pp.234f. Some commentators see in this speech traces of a meeting of the non-Catholic advisers, but probably wrongly, since this was not about the specific topic of the 'hierarchy of truths' (personal communication from Giuseppe Alberigo). Pangrazio's archdiocese of Gorizia is now on Italian territory and borders on Slovenia, which at the time of the Council was Yugoslavia. At the time of the Austro-Hungarian monarchy, i.e. until 1918, Gorizia was the metropolis of the largely Slovenian church province which went under the name of Görz; Pangrazio, who was born in Budapest in 1909, had thus since 1909 been archbishop in the nationally and confessionally explosive triangle of land between Italy, Yugoslavia and Austria. That perhaps explains his unusual ecumenical sensitivity.

14. For the state of official church understanding in this and other questions see the solid survey in Heinz Schütte, *Ziel: Kirchengemeinschaft. Zur Ökumenischen Orientierung*, Paderborn 1985; id., *Kirche im ökumenischen Verstandnis. Kirche des dreieinigen Gottes*, Paderbom 1991; cf. also the sketch of the problems and representative literature in Otto Hermann Pesch, 'Heisse Eisen der Ökumene im Spiegel ökumenischer Probleme des Alltags', in Konrad Raiser and Dorothea Sattler (eds), *Ökumene vor neuen Zeiten. Für Theodor Schneider*, Freiburg im Breisgau 2000, pp.441–74.

15. It is precisely here that the questionable character of the assertion in the declaration *Dominus Iesus* no. 17, becomes evident, that churches which do not have the 'means' of an episcopal constitution in the customary Catholic understanding, i.e. that which has grown up in history, are 'not proper churches'. Is that not making the means an end?

16. Cf. for the moment Otto Hermann Pesch, 'Epilog zur Ekklesiologie', in *Ökumenische Rundschau* 46, 1997, pp.284–302. in the background is Yves Congar, 'Die Wesenseigenschaften der Kirche', in Johannes Feiner and Magnus Uhrer (eds), *Mysterium Salutis. Grundriss heilsgeschichtlicher Dogmatik*, Vol. 4/1, Zurich 1972, pp.357–599: 368–410; and Ulrich Kühn, *Kirche*, Gütersloh 1980, pp.164–201; Medard Kehl, *Die Kirche. Eine katholische Ekklesiologie*, Würzburg ³1994, pp.103–31, 181–210, 388–402.

17. There is a short survey of the problem and a bibliography in Fries and Pesch (see n.6), p.174; Otto Hermann Pesch, '"Ökumenischer Imperialismus"? Grundsätzliche Überlegungen zu den Auswirkungen grosskirchlicher bilateraler Gespräche auf die Kleinen Kirchen und kirchlichen Gemeinschaften', in Wolfgang Beinert, Konrad Feiereis and Hemann-Josef Röhring (eds), *Unterwegs zum einem Glauben. Festschrift für Lothar Ullrich*, Leipzig 1997, pp.561–78: 575ff.

18. There is an assessment of the extremely lively discussion in Otto Hermann Pesch, 'Gemeinschaft beim Herrenmahl. Plädoyer für ein Ende der Denkverweigerungen', in Bernd Jochen Hilberath and Dorothea Sattler (eds), *Vorgeschmack. Ökumenische Bemühungen um die Eucharistie. Festschrift für Theodor Schneider*, Mainz 1995, pp.539–71.

19. Cf. the subtle and sober investigation by Horst Gorski, *Die Niedrigkeit seiner Magd. Darstellung und theologische Analyse der Mariologie Martin Luthers als Beitrag zum gegenwärtigen lutherisch/römisch-katholischen Gespräch*, Frankfurt am Main and Bern 1987.

20. Wilhelm de Vries, 'Die Entwicklung des Primats in den ersten drei Jahrhunderten', in Arbeitsgemeinschaft ökumenischer Universitätsinstitute (ed), *Papstum als ökumenische Frage*, Munich and Mainz 1979, pp.114–33; there is now a summary with bibliography in Klaus Schatz, 'Papst', I–II, in *LThK³*, Vol.7, pp.1327–31. Does the special emphasis on the episcopate in the Eastern church despite the synodical traditions rest on that?

21. Cf. Dorothea Wendebourg, 'Das Amt und die Ämter', *Zeitschrift für evangelisches Kirchenrecht* 45, 2000, pp.5–37. This representative Lutheran contribution should be read with Catholic eyes 'against the grain' to see the possibilities for a 'differentiated consensus' on church ministry.

22. Cf. Lukas Vischer, 'Wie weiter – nach den ersten zehn Jahren?, in Gerard Békés and Vilmos Vajta (eds), *Unitatis redintegratio 1964–1974. Eine Bilanz der Auswirkungen des Ökumenismusdekretes*, Frankfurt am Main 1977, pp.141–57.

Towards an Ecumenical Interpretation of the Code of Canon Law of the Latin Catholic Church

ALPHONSE BORRAS

How can 'ecumenical structures', i.e. structures which allow exchanges at the deepest level and which accelerate the way towards unity, be generated in the churches? In this connection I want to examine the possibilities offered by the Code of Canon Law of the Latin Catholic Church, which was promulgated in 1983. Despite the limits imposed on this article, first it is necessary to remind ourselves of some doctrinal issues before entering some specific areas in which the 1983 Code can encourage both Latin Catholics and their dioceses and other ecclesiastical constituencies to put communion with other churches into practice.[1] I will try to present some 'practical' perspectives without denying the difficulties and the obstacles involved, even if it is impossible to treat them theologically here.

I. Introductory remarks

1. The 1983 Code is beyond question a major canonical document of the Roman Catholic Church. But canon law cannot be reduced to the Code. The Code contains the essential regulations which apply to the Latin church (cf. c.1). Other regulations issued by the Apostolic See in Rome are equally in force for Catholics of the Latin rite, if not for all others. In other words, the Code does not contain the whole of universal law.

2. Moreover, ecumenically speaking, the 1983 Code and its equivalent for the Eastern Catholic Churches promulgated in 1990 were followed in 1993 by a new Ecumenical Directory, which brought up to date the previous one published in two parts in 1967 and 1970 respectively.[2] Formally speaking, such a directory is a general executory decree (cf. c.31§1). Thus it spells out the ordinances of the 1983 and 1990 Codes and urges their observation. By virtue of this, it must be considered an *authentic* commentary on the law by the legislator himself. Consequently, a complete examination of the 1983

Code must be made in the light of the 1993 Directory. Readers will therefore have to supplement their study of the Latin Code with the stipulations of the Directory, to which I will simply refer.

3. The Code also refers to the particular right of the dioceses and other jurisdictional entities which can make laws in connection with ecumenism. At the risk of anticipating the consequences of my proposals, it is worth saying here that the rise of 'ecumenical structures' falls principally to the particular law of the dioceses and, failing that, the conferences of bishops. Thus the reader needs to be aware of this indispensable extension of the Code by specific laws. The Directory itself invites this. Moreover, it aims 'fully to represent the competencies of authorities at different levels' of the church which are the particular churches and their groupings, among other things the conferences of bishops (no.6).

4. A fourth remark reminds us that church law, whether universal or particular, is not everything in the life of the Catholic church. It is a specifically juridical regulation of ecclesial life. It is not the whole of the life of the church, but in the form of general and abstract dispositions it 'provides for' a good ecclesial order which respects the dignity of persons and the nature of institutions not only *ratione iusti* but above all with a view to the promotion of ecclesial communion. From this juridical perspective, the law is primarily concerned with the validity of juridic acts. This is notably the case in connection with the sacraments.[3] A juridic act will be qualified as 'valid' on the threefold condition 'that it be placed by a person capable of placing it, and that it include those elements which essentially constitute it as well as the formalities and requisites imposed by law for the validity of the act' (c.124§1). The validity of a juridic act is equivalent to its efficacy, i.e. the production of the effect aimed at.[4] So canonical discourse is preoccupied with the 'juridic' effects of human acts, i.e. their incidence on the legal scene in connection both with the obligations and the rights of individuals and communities. A juridic act is either valid or not; there is no third possibility. In canon law a eucharist, for example, is either a valid sacrament or it is not. By contrast, theology investigates the nature or at least the 'theological' scope of the life of people and communities. For example, it will study what constitutes the eucharistic mystery to identify in it what has been more or less fully preserved. Theologically speaking, a number of gradations are therefore possible: we no longer have the alternative of 'all or nothing'. In other words, to note juridic invalidity is not necessarily to deny theological reality.

5. Then it is important to distinguish between canonical and theological discourse. That is my fifth point. This distinction derives from their respec-

tive approaches to the real, the *ratio sub qua* from which they consider it: theology is situated at the level of that which is; canon law at the level of what must be. The former describes; the latter prescribes. Canon law sets *limits* to the action of the faithful. But it cannot in any way deny the nature of things and the density of reality, which theology examines to grasp what we are told about human beings, God and his covenant, the meaning of human destiny and the history of humankind. The 'ecumenical structures' *delimited* by canonical discourse will always fall short of the wealth of ecclesial life and theological revelation. The canonical 'delimitations' do not necessarily prejudge a lack of theological and practical consistency.

6. Canonical interpretation cannot disregard a theological understanding, to which it refers at least implicitly. Now the 1983 Code was presented by John Paul II as an attempt to translate Vatican II into law. That is my sixth remark. That gives rise to the fundamental hermeneutical principle that it is not Vatican II which must be referred to the Code but vice versa: 'the Code must always be referred to this image (the conciliar image of the church) as the primary pattern whose outline the Code ought to express in so far as it can by its very nature'.[5] Here the ecclesiology of the council performs the function of the metatext which prevents the closure of the canonical texts of the Code. Among these doctrinal elements of Vatican II encountered by the Code, as well as the church understood as *communion* there is the commitment to ecumenism (SDL, p.XIII). The 1993 Directory recalls that the quest for the unity of Christians was 'one of the principal concerns' of Vatican II (cf. no.1). Ecclesial communion rooted in baptism and anchored in the life of the Trinity cannot be reduced to communion in the Catholic church alone, since the church of Christ cannot be reduced to this; however, it does subsist in it, albeit not in an exclusive way (cf. LG 8b and UR 3c, 4b; chs 11 and 205§2).[6] The subsistence of the church of Christ in the Catholic church signifies a non-exclusive identity and at the same time the irreducibility of the mystery of the church. It follows that the sacraments are not exclusively the sacraments of the unity of the Catholic church alone. Thus the 'ecumenical structures' to be promoted must draw the canonical conclusions from the transition from an *exclusive* identity (the church of Christ is the Catholic church) to an *inclusive* identity (the church of Christ subsists in the Catholic church).

7. Since the last council, the Catholic church has sweepingly designated the other churches by the double expression 'other churches and ecclesial communities'.[7] These different appellations rest on a recognition of the ecclesiality of the other collectivities (Latin *coetus christianorum*, cf. UR 13d).[8] Canonically speaking these could be approached from the concept

of *ecclesia sui iuris*, a 'church with its own law', according to the stipulative definition given by the Code of Canons of the Eastern Catholic Churches (= CCEO): 'The group of faithful Christians united by the hierarchy according to law, which the supreme authority of the church recognizes explicitly or tacitly as its own law, is called a church with its own law in the recent code' (c. 27).[9] In the event, the concept of *ecclesia sui iuris* would serve as a model which is both heuristic and practical, i.e. for *understanding* these ecclesial realities (and locating them in the Catholic church) and acting consistently towards them (and hence locating *oneself* in relation to them). These churches and ecclesial communities are *de facto* explicitly 'recognized' as such by the supreme authority of the Catholic church both in the conciliar texts and in later documents. Moreover current ecumenical documents have already tacitly arrived at such a recognition. The ancient Eastern churches and the Orthodox churches correspond to the concept of the *ecclesia sui iuris*. This concept will sometimes be more difficult to apply to the churches arising out of the Reformation. For example, the Anglican Communion comprises autonomous provinces, and the majority of the great churches are federated on a global plan although their elements, often national, enjoy complete autonomy.

II. Some canonical perspectives on 'ecumenical structures'

The 1983 Code contains dispositions relevant to relations with non-Catholic Christians and determines their obligations and rights and those of Catholic faithful in ecumenical matters.[10] However, these relations and the bonds which arise from them lie on a mainly individual level between the persons concerned. The exchange is of a spiritual kind and only incidentally takes confessional references into account. That, at least, is the point of view of the Code, which does not go on specifically to consider the ecclesiological consistency of the church or ecclesial community.[11] From a canonical point of view these relations between the faithful of churches which are not yet in full communion will *in principle* give place to a rapprochement between the baptized. They will even contribute towards forging links between their respective communities. But they are not open to their mutual recognition. The spiritual exchange between the baptized does not extend as far as ecclesial concord between their communities.

The dispositions of the Code do not envisage this stage of a visible interecclesial unity. Certainly the Code concerns only Catholics (c.11). It is not competent to legislate in domains which similarly relate to the specific law of the other churches and ecclesial communities. Nevertheless the 1983 Code authorizes – in the twofold sense of 'allow' and 'endorse' – acts (individual acts and collective activities) which, going beyond rapprochment between Christians, already point towards the visible unity between the churches. In this sense certain canons can be considered fundamental references for 'ecumenical structures' within the dioceses or conferences of bishops. I personally see above all three specific domains where deeper exchanges can be encouraged by these structures and give institutional form to the growing communion with other churches.

1. The responsibility of diocesan bishops and conferences of bishops

Having affirmed that 'it is within the special competence of the entire college of bishops and of the Apostolic See to promote and direct the participation of Catholics in the ecumenical movement' (c.755§1), the Code stipulates that it is for bishops and, in accordance with the law, conferences of bishops to promote the unity of Christians and, when occasion arises, to issue appropriate practical rules, taking account of the instructions issued by the supreme church authority (§2). The 1993 Directory, the authentic interpreter of the Code, has moreover explicitly recalled that a Catholic diocese or several dioceses 'acting closely together' will be 'in a very favourable position' for establishing with other churches or ecclesial communities 'fruitful ecumenical relations which contribute to the wider ecumenical movement' (no.38, cf. nos.166–71). In this connection the Directory recalls the responsibility of the diocesan bishops individually and that of the conferences of bishops to 'establish norms according to which persons or commissions . . . are to carry out the activities ascribed to them and to oversee the implementation of these norms' (no.40).

On the diocesan level, this role of actively promoting the ecumenical movement will be assumed by a diocesan officer who, in close collaboration with the bishop, will represent the diocese in its relations with the other churches and ecclesial communities and their authorities 'and will facilitate contacts between the latter and the local bishop of the place, clergy and laity on various levels' (no.41).[12] Even where Catholics are in a majority or their resources are somewhat poor, the Directory warmly recommends the designation of a diocesan officer (ibid.).

For the promotion of ecumenical activity and the implementation of 'practical rules' (cf. c.755§2) the Directory provides for the creation of 'a council, commission or secretariat' (no.42). Within this organ, which will reflect the diversity of the diocese, 'it is desirable that representatives of the presbyterial council, the pastoral council, diocesan or regional seminaries be included among the members of the commission or secretariat' (no.43a). It is good to note the emphasis on co-operation with other ecumenical authorities, the help to be given to the diocesan officer and the support for initiatives on the ground. In addition to its function on the level of spiritual ecumenism and mutual charity, this diocesan organ must take the initiative and direct ecumenical conversations or consultations, and promote a common witness to the faith in different spheres (no.44). The particular law must encourage the parishes to take ecumenical initiatives 'on their own level' and create groups responsible for implementing them (45). Echoing what the Code prescribes as being among the obligations of the diocesan bishop, namely the promotion of ecumenism (cf. c.383§3), the Directory takes responsibility for 'the forms and structures of ecumenical collaboration', in these terms: 'Ultimately, it is for the diocesan bishop, taking account of what has been decided at the regional or national level, to judge the acceptability and appropriateness of all forms of local ecumenical action' (no.164).

At the level of conferences of bishops the Directory provides for an episcopal commission for ecumenism supported by experts and, if need be, assisted by a permanent secretariat (no.46). It has many functions: the list of its tasks is in no way exhaustive (cf. 'some examples', no.47). Among others I have noted that it has to 'establish consultations and dialogue with church leaders and with councils of churches which exist on a national or territorial (as distinct from the diocesan) level provide suitable structures for these dialogues' (no.47e). Ecumenical collaboration, spiritual exchange to the point of common witness, will be organizationally ensured by the councils of churches and Christian councils which 'are among the more permanent structures that are set up for promoting unity and ecumenical collaboration' (no.166).

These ecumenical structures call for a firm effort to train the faithful and the communities. Following the Code, which speaks of the 'concern for ecumenical questions' to be raised during the training of seminarians (cf. c.256§2), the Directory certainly deals with the training of those who work in the pastoral ministry, clergy and laity (nos.70–86),[13] but it also touches on the training of all Catholics (nos 58–69) and envisages both specialized (nos 87–90) and permanent training (no.91).

2. *Specific legislation on communicatio in sacris*

Communicatio in sacris on the sacramental level is regulated by the instructions of canon 844. This is not the place to comment on its content.[14] In the event, the Directory presents itself as the authentic interpreter of these instructions.[15] The Directory considers *communicatio in sacris* to be a contribution 'to the growth of harmony among Christians' (no.105). It even envisages the possibilities of a legitimate reciprocity which would be the result of 'consultations between appropriate Catholic authorities and those of other communions'[16] (no.106). One of the objectives of these consultations will be 'a greater mutual understanding of each other's discipline, and even an agreement on how to manage a situation in which the discipline of one church calls into question or conflicts with the discipline of another' (no.107).

Canon 844§5 mentions the general norms enacted by the diocesan bishop or the conference of bishops relating to the different situations mentioned previously, in particular necessity or spiritual advantage (§2), perhaps impossible situations (§2–4), the request for non-Catholics in particular circumstances (§3–4), cases of grave and urgent necessity (§4).[17] These rules will not be made 'except after consultation with at least the local competent authority of the interested non-Catholic church or community' (§5).[18] It will be a matter of establishing norms which are general in nature – under the form of particular law (c.13), the decree (c.29), even instruction or rule (c.34) – for situations of grave and pressing need and 'verifying the conditions where it is impossible to have recourse to a non-Catholic ministry' (Directory nos 130 and 131). These norms concern cases of grave and urgent necessity (comparable to the danger of death as in persecution, imprisonment or even a Diaspora situation) involving the non-Catholic faithful of other churches and ecclesial communities like the Eastern churches or their equivalents (CIC c. 844§4).[19]

The *communicatio in sacris* ratified by the 1983 Code and its authentic interpreter, the 1993 Directory, rests on an individual approach to sacramental sharing. But it does not do away with a confessional approach, since it honours the ecclesiological consistency of the church or ecclesial community *a quo* by asking about the validity of the sacrament or the adhesion to the Catholic faith of those concerned. It nevertheless falls short of an ecclesiogenetic approach to sacramental sharing entered into *with discernment* 'to re-establish the unity of Christians' (cf. UR 8d).[20]

3. The reality of interchurch families

Interchurch families form an original ecclesial situation which hands on the heritage of a division and at the same time gives the pledge of a re-establishment of unity. Their witness can contribute towards directing all towards unity, even if these matrimonial situations present their own diffi-culties.[21] Pastors must ensure 'that the Catholic spouse and the children born of a mixed marriage do not lack spiritual assistance in fulfilling their obligations and are to aid the spouses in fostering the unity of conjugal and family life' (c.1128). If the non-Catholic spouse is Eastern, given the 'very close communion in matters of faith' between his or her church and the Catholic church (Directory no.122) it is canon 844§3 which applies (cf. no.125). The Catholic spouse of an Eastern Christian can go to the sacra-ments in the Eastern churches in conformity with canon 844§2 (cf. nos.123–4). On the other hand, by virtue of canon 844§4, taking part in the sacrament is more limited when one of the two spouses comes from a Reformation church.

However, the Directory envisages particular situations which allow the admission of the non-Catholic spouse to eucharistic communion (nos 159 and 160).[22] The first situation can arise at the eucharist in connection with a marriage which, while not advised, can be allowed by the diocesan bishop 'for a just reason' (no.159). It provides that the decision to admit the non-Catholic party to eucharistic communion will be made in accord with general norms in the matter, namely the spontaneous request of the non-Catholic party, the same belief in the eucharist and the required dispositions (c.844§4). The situation envisaged here by the Directory is an additional exception to those given by canon 844§§2–4. The non-Catholic is admitted to communion because in this situation he or she cannot have recourse to the ministry of their own church or ecclesial community.

The other specific situations seem to be a kind of watermark in the Directory (no.160). While recalling the exceptional character of eucharistic sharing, the Directory provides, for example, for the situation of spouses who are authentically living out their Christian faith in their commitment as a couple with a home (cf. no.145). Or again, the eucharistic sharing could take place in important events in the life of the couple or the family as, for example, the baptism of children into the Catholic church, their first com-munion or their confirmation, not to mention events affecting relatives or friends like an ordination or a religious profession. One could even think of a parish family event, a significant ecumenical encounter for the interested parties, or again a retreat or a recollection experienced as a couple or a family.[23]

The basis for the possible openings lies specifically in taking seriously the domestic church which is formed by the family (cf. LG 11b; AA 11d). In the event, this is a sign of the unity which is already really given in Christ and the promise of what will come when God is fully all in all. Furthermore it is an original ecclesial setting which as such calls for participation in the means of grace not simply or primarily for individual needs but for basically ecclesiological reasons, namely the edification of this *ecclesia domestica.* This task proves to be a 'grave and urgent necessity', first of all for the spouses but above all for the children. Canonically, such exceptions will also require the authorization of the bishop.[24] Doctrinally, they suggest to us that there is room for undertaking a basically ecclesiological (and not just spiritual!)[25] reflection on the interchurch family as a domestic church, in conformity with the great ecumenical affirmations of the last council.

III. Conclusion

The 'ecumenical structures' aimed at deepening the exchanges between churches and hastening reconciliation between them are based on a real, though imperfect, communion which they have ceaselessly to promote and to increase, in the hope that the Lord will grant full communion in the faith, the sacraments, the ministries and church life. They encourage the development of a real inter-ecclesial fabric between the Catholic church and the other churches and ecclesial communities. The canonical mechanism does not just point to the unity of Christians but to the unity of the churches. This unity is certainly inchoate in a tension between a certain unity already signified and participation in the means of grace, i.e. between the sign of a grace already received (*which already creates the unity*) and the means of a grace which is to be received (*to achieve this unity*).

Even more than the 1983 Code, the 1993 Directory, its authentic interpreter, emphasizes the particular law. The efficacy of the canons of the Code will eventually be a function of the vitality of the specific law of diocesan and episcopal conferences. It is mainly at the level of the particular churches and their grouping that these ecumenical advances need to be made. They will live on with the churches and ecclesial communities if there is scope to consider them *ecclesiae sui iuris*, namely groups of faithful with their respective hierarchies according to their own law.

Translated by John Bowden

Notes

1. In connection with a subject as vast and complex as this, it is worth studying L. Pivonka, 'The Revised Code of Canon Law: Ecumenical Implications', *The Jurist* 45, 1985, pp.521–48.

2. Pontifical Council for Promoting the Unity of Christians, *Directory for the Application of Principles and Norms on Ecumenism* (= 1993 Directory). This Document is a revised text of the Ecumenical Directory called for during Vatican II and published in two parts, one in 1967 and the other in 1970.

3. Cf. P. M. Gy, 'La validité sacramentelle/ Développement de la notion avant le Concile de Trent', in *La Liturgie dans l'histoire*, Paris 1990, pp.165–75.

4. If an action does not produce the juridical effects envisaged because of the absence of one of the conditions provided for by c.124§2, it is invalid. This invalidity can arise in two ways: either the act does not exist from a juridical point of view or it is outside the law and its efficacy (cf. c.10). Cf. F. J. Urrutia, *Les normes générales,. Commentaire des canons 1–203*, Le Nouveau Droit ecclésial, Paris 1994, pp.202–3.

5. John Paul II, Apostolic Constitution *Sacrae disciplinae leges* (= SDL), in *Code of Canon Law: Latin-English Edition*, Washington DC 1983, p.xiv.

6. Cf. V. I. Papez, 'Diritto canonico ed ecumenismo', in *Pontificium Consilium de Legum Textibus Interpretandis, Ius in vita et in missione Ecclesiae*, Vatican City 1994, pp.1190–3.

7. Cf. LG 15, UR 13–24; 1993 Directory nos 122–36: 133. Note that the fathers of the council generally write these expressions with capitals (cf. e.g. UR 19b; by contrast, LG 15 writes 'communities' lower case).

8. The concrete application of one or other term is precisely the function of the degree of visible communion in terms of the threefold register which is mentioned immediately (cf. UR 21; CIC 1983, c.205) according to the 'many elements of sanctification and truth' recognized by the Catholic church in themselves and which 'as gifts proper to the church of Christ are forces impelling towards Catholic unity' (LG 8b, cf. UR b, c, d). No.104b of the Directory refers in a note to some Vatican texts which are particularly important in this connection, e.g. LG 8 and UR 3–4 for the ecclesiological value of the non-Catholic churches and ecclesial communities (cf. nn. 115 and 116) and UR 3, 15, 22 for the value of their celebrations for the life of grace and access to the communion of salvation (cf. n.117).

9. According to J.-C. Perisset, who had this good idea, the non-Catholic churches and ecclesial communities are in fact *sui iuris*: over and above the elements of sanctification and truth, they are organized according to their own laws (cf. *Latin ut sui iuris*, CCEO c.21): they are linked to a hierarchy (cf. Latin *coetus hierarchia iunctus*), even if they do not all have 'pastors' in the sense that the Roman Catholic church attaches to this word, namely an ordained ministry, the episcopate *par excellence*, as a sign and guarantee of ecclesial apostolicity. A large number of ecclesial communities exercise, rather, ecclesial ministry in a collegial form. Cf. J.-C. Perisset, 'Le implicazioni ecumeniche del diritto canonico e le implicazioni canoniche dell'ecumenismo', *Periodica* 88, 1999, pp.61–90, here pp.64–7.

10. Cf. for example c.463§ 3 (invitation of non-Catholic observers to the diocesan

synod), c.755 (duties of the college of bishops on ecumenism), c. 825§2 (joint publication of translations of the Bible), c. 844 (*communicatio in sacris*), c. 869§2 (recognition of baptism), c. 874§2 (the sponsor at the baptism of a Catholic), c. 933 (eucharistic celebration in a non-Catholic church), c. 1183§3 (non-Catholic funeral), 1124–9 (mixed marriages), etc. Cf. Pivonka, 'The Revised Code of Canon Law: Ecumenical Implications' (n.1), 530–47.

11. It would be like a threefold register, individual, confessional and ecclesial, of the exchange of spiritual goods and rapprochement between the churches forming so to speak three approaches which are in principle linked together. These three levels are correlative: the reception of grace is certainly individual or subjective, but it cannot be separated from ecclesial rapprochement; personal encounter with God cannot be separated from encounter with the other believers who share in the fruits of salvation; and this level implies or calls for a common confession. My canon-law colleague in Mainz speaks of 'forms' (individual, confessional representative) of *communicatio in sacris*. Cf. I. Ridel-Spangenberger, '*Communicatio in sacris*. Zur Korrelation zwischen geistlicher und kirchlicher Gemeinschaft in ökumenischen und rechtsgeschichtlichen Bezügen', in B. J. Hilberath and D. Sattler (eds), *Vorgeschmack. Ökumenische Bemühungen um die Eucharistie, Festschrift für Theodor Schneider*, Mainz 1995, pp.482–500.

12. The diocesan official is competent to encourage initiatives in prayers for unity in the diocese, to see that 'ecumenical attitudes' influence the activities of the diocese, to identify and to supply its particular needs (ibid.). The true ecumenical counsellor of the bishop and other diocesan authorities, he will 'facilitate the sharing of ecumenical experiences and initiatives with pastors and diocesan organizations' (ibid.). His role is also to 'maintain contact with officers or commissions of other dioceses' (ibid.).

13. Cf. the document of the Pontifical Council for Promoting Christian Unity, 'La dimension oecuménique de la formation de ceux qui travaillent dans le ministère pastoral', *DC* 95, 1998, pp.455–64.

14. For the eucharist see my study: A. Borras, 'L'Église catholique et la *communicatio in sacris* relative à l'eucharistie', *Irenikon* 72, 1999/3–4, pp.365–434.

15. The Directory is an example of an interpretation of the Code on the basis of Vatican II, the major doctrinal positions of which it integrates, whatever opinion one may have on the openness or the dispositions which it contains. Like the 1983 and 1990 Codes it has at least drawn conclusions from the differentiated degree of ecclesial communion to establish and interpret authentically the canonical norms corresponding to the actual limits of sacramental sharing.

16. Note the use of the term 'Communion' in capitals as a global designation for the other churches or ecclesial communities.

17. If in the 1917 Code the *communicatio in sacris* with non-Catholics was considered a danger to the unity of the church signified by the sacraments, if not its negation, from now on it is no longer necessarily considered to put this unity in danger. The very rare and limited exceptions of the past (CIC 1917, c.1258 §2,

cf. c.2261 §2) have been succeeded by a range of exceptions aimed at the spiritual good of the interested party and by virtue of the greater or lesser visible communion of his or her church or ecclesiastical community with the Catholic church (CIC 1983, c.844; CCEO, c.672).

18. The Latin conjunction *aut* seems to indicate an alternative. It is nothing of the sort if one refers to the Directory, which gives preference to the diocesan (or eparchial) bishop. He is to establish general norms 'taking into account any norms which may have been established for this matter by the episcopal conference or by the synods of Eastern Catholic churches' (no.130). Note also that the Directory says 'after consultation with at least the competent authority of the other church or ecclesial community' (ibid.).

19. Once the general norms have been established, it is for the diocesan bishop or the ordinary of the place in question to assess each particular case. The 1993 Directory goes further by mentioning in general the 'Catholic ministers' who are 'to judge particular cases and to administer these sacraments only in accord with these established norms, where they exist. Otherwise they will judge according to the norms of this Directory' (no.130 end).

20. If the Directory had not clearly drawn the disciplinary conclusions from an understanding of the sacraments as 'sources of unity' (no.129a), its dispositions would have represented a more dynamic articulation of the individual and confessional approaches to eucharistic hospitality. Cf. Ridel-Spangenberger, '*Communicatio in sacris*. Zur Korrelation zwischen geistlicher und kirchlicher Gemeinschaft in ökumenischer und rechtsgeschichtlicher Bezügen' (n.11), p.499.

21. Directory no. 145, citing John Paul II, post-synodal apostolic exhortation *Familiaris consortio* no.89. The difficulties bound up with the fact of not sharing in a full visible communion in the faith and the sacraments and in ecclesial life can affect the perfect union of persons and the community of life and destiny between them, *consortium totius vitae* (cf. CIC c. 1055§1; Directory no.144).

22. Depending on the context, the dispositions of nos 159 and 160 apply to Christians of Reformation churches and ecclesial communities, even if there is mention of the observance of the general norms for Eastern Christians (cf. the reference of no.125). Cf. Perisset, 'Le implicazioni ecumeniche del diritto canonico e le implicazioni canoniche dell'ecumenismo' (n.9), p.84.

23. To complicate things, Perisset asks whether such exceptions are valid in the case of a marriage concluded with a dispensation from canonical forms (c.1117§2): 'Since these exceptions exist, for reasons which the Catholic spouse has not been able to overcome, they should not condition the life of the family in the sense that the spouses were considered less 'faithful to the canonical implications of ecumenism', p.86.

24. Cf. the reference by Directory no.160 to nos. 125, 130, 131, corresponding to c.844§§3 and 4.

25. Cf. K. Raiser, 'Églises de maison', *Foyers mixtes* 124, 1999, pp.6–7.

Ecumenical Openings in the Code of Canons of the Eastern Churches

ASTRID KAPTIJN

It is significant that the principles and dispositions enunciated by Vatican II in relation to the other Christian churches and ecclesial communities which we find in the decrees *Unitatis Redintegratio* on ecumenism and *Orientalium Ecclesiarum*, which relates to the Eastern Catholic churches, are a factor in the revision of the two Codes of the Catholic church which Pope John XXIII had announced. Both texts can be associated with the basic principle of *Lumen Gentium* 8 that the church of Christ is to be found in the Catholic church.[1] This work of revision began after Vatican II and took the work of the council as its basis. However, there was no time to draw conclusions from this change of perspective, and the practice of the Roman Curia and the canonical norms issued in the period after the council are evidence of this. We can even ask whether the Catholic church has already integrated into its canon law all the consequences of the conciliar spirit as far as the other Christian churches and ecclesial communities are concerned. For the moment, however, we shall examine the oppportunities for relations with non-Catholic churches and ecclesial communities formulated by one of the two Codes, the Code relating to the Eastern Catholic churches, which was promulgated in 1990.[2]

Introduction: an ecumenical aspect upheld

We note that the ecumenical aspect of the Code of Canons of the Eastern Churches (*Codex Canonum Ecclesiarum Orientalium* = CCEO) was emphasized from the start of the revision of the canon law of these churches. One of the guiding principles formulated to direct the work of revision, and approved by commission on the revision in March 1974, already spoke of the ecumenical character of this future Code, emphasizing the mission of the Eastern Catholic churches relating to the 'special duty of promoting the unity of all Christians'.[3] Then the commission advised that '. . . where the

Orthodox Churches are concerned, the Code must be inspired by the words of Paul VI on the "sister churches" and their "*almost full*" communion, and the respect due to the hierarchs of these churches, who are to be regarded as "pastors to whom part of Christ's flock has been entrusted", and by the conciliar text which deals with the right of these churches to "govern themselves according to their own disciplines, since these are better suited to the character of their faithful and better adapted to foster the good of souls" (*Unitatis Redintegratio* 16)'.[4]

In the apostolic constitution *Sacri canones* by which Pope John Paul II promulgated the CCEO, the pope emphasized this very mission of the Eastern Catholic churches, reinforced by the fact that they share with the Eastern churches which are not yet in full communion with the Catholic church the same unique heritage of canonical discipline. He declared that the most serious reason for abrogating the laws of this Code in the long run would certainly be 'the reason of full communion of all the Eastern churches with the Catholic church, which moreover corresponds perfectly to the desire of our saviour Jesus Christ himself'. [5] One can also cite what the Holy Father said on 25 October 1990 in his presentation of the CCEO to the synod of bishops: 'To all the Orthodox churches also, I would like to "present" this Code which, from the beginning of work on it, has been conceived and developed on the basis of principles of true ecumenism, and in very first place the great esteem which the church professes for its sister churches . . .'[6]

Thus the ecumenical perspective specifically guided the revision of CCEO. At the same time, the privileged place accorded to the Orthodox churches among the non-Catholic churches and ecclesial communities has often been repeated.

A first glance at the content of CCEO brings out this ecumenical aspect: there is a title of CCEO which is entirely devoted to the subject, but the Code does not stop at that.[7]

I. Promoting ecumenism

The desire to encourage an ecumenical spirit is expressed several times in CCEO. The title 'Ecumenism or the Promotion of Christian Unity' begins: 'As the concern to bring about the unity of all Christians is one of the whole church, all Christian faithful, above all the pastors of the church, must pray for this full unity of the church desired by the Lord and work on it, participating cleverly in the ecumenical work aroused by the grace of the Holy Spirit.'[8] What is striking here is the fact that the promotion of the unity of

Christians is primarily presented as a concern of the whole church: mention is first made of all the Christian faithful and only then of the pastors of the church. Secondly, it relates to divine law, for the re-establishment of unity is *desired by the Lord*. Then it takes up the Vatican II texts which emphasize the special charge on the Eastern Catholic churches to encourage the unity of all the Eastern churches.[9] However, open and confident ecumenical dialogue and common initiatives with other Christians call for caution, so that 'the dangers of a false irenism, indifferentism and an excessive zeal'[10] are avoided.

To encourage ecumenical initiatives it is prescribed that each Eastern Catholic church, designated by the term 'church with its own law',[11] will formulate norms of particular law specific to each of these churches and have a commission of experts on ecumenism. Each eparchy, or possible several eparchies together, must have a council for the promotion of the ecumenical movement.[12] If that cannot be done, there must be at least a Christian faithful in each eparchy who has been nominated for this task.[13] The preachers, those who are in charge of the means of social communication, and teachers and directors of Catholic schools and institutions of further education, must make known the teaching and tradition of the Catholic church and those of the other churches or ecclesial communities.[14] Finally, the last canon under this title expresses the desire that Catholics should collaborate as far as possible with other Christians, 'particularly in the works of charity and social justice, the defence of the dignity of the human person and its fundamental rights, the promotion of peace, national days of commemoration and national festivals', while observing the rules about communication in the sacred things.[15]

CCEO also emphasizes the task of the eparchial bishop in seeing that the faithful entrusted to his care encourage unity among Christians according to the principles approved by the church.[16] Then the pastor must give 'the example of truly priestly and pastoral ministry to the baptized and the non-baptized, to Catholics and non-Catholics'.[17] We also find prescriptions which integrate ecumenism into the training of seminarians[18] and catechesis.[19]

In a more concrete way, an attempt is made to respect certain rights of baptized non-Catholics by a norm which prescribes: 'The directors of schools, hospitals and all other similar Catholic institutions are to see that the other Christians who attend these institutions or reside in them can obtain spiritual help and receive the sacraments from their own ministers.'[20] Special attention is paid to Catholic schools. The characteristic of these schools, like the obligation to create a scholarly ambience inspired by the gospel spirit of freedom and love; to help young people to develop their personalities in such a way as to bring about growth in the new creation which they have become by baptism; and to ensure that their knowledge of the world and human life are illuminated by faith, must be adapted to circumstances if the majority of the pupils at the school are not Catholics.[21]

We note that these canons of CCEO not only express the furthering of Christian unity as a pious vow but also designate the organisms and categories of the faithful which must be specially concerned with it, along with fields of common action. Respect for the ecclesial allegiance of other Christians is especially emphasized by the specific ruling that they must have access to the spiritual goods provided by the ministers of their churches, even if they are in Catholic institutions.[22]

II. Some basic principles

CCEO contains some basic principles, arising from the new perspective of Vatican II, which guide relations with non-Catholic Christians. We already note the change in terminology from the time before the council. Although the term 'baptized non-Catholics' is retained, the term 'churches or ecclesial communities which are not yet in full communion with the Catholic church' is also used.[23] Moreover it is specified first of all that this Code concerns only the Eastern Catholic churches[24] and that from now on non-baptized Catholics are no longer governed by purely ecclesiastical laws.[25] Not only are the ecclesiastical laws of the Catholic church no longer applied to non-Catholic Christians, but their own law or discipline is also respected. Two canons of CCEO are very explicit on this subject. They are worth quoting in their entirety, all the more so since they have no equivalent in the Latin Code. They are both concerned with marriage law. Canon 780§2 stipulates: 'The marriage between a Catholic party and a non-Catholic baptized party, divine law being safeguarded, is also governed: 1. By the specific law of the church or the ecclesial community to which the non-Catholic party belongs, if this community has its own marriage law; 2. By the law by which the non-Catholic party is bound if the church community to which he or she belongs does not have its own marriage law.' In other words, if the church or ecclesial community has its own marriage law, the Catholic church respects it; if not, there is necessarily another law by which the person is bound – usually one thinks of the civil law of the country. But in both these cases the laws are respected only to the degree that they are compatible with divine law.

Canonists have asked whether or not the law of other churches and ecclesial communities can apply to all aspects of marriage. A common opinion seems to be emerging in canonical doctrine that these other laws are applied only in connection with the juridical capacity of each person, in other words, in connection with the question of hindrances to marriage (and clearly this is always under the provision of divine law), but not in questions of defective consent, the dissolution of the bond or the simple or radical convalidation of the marriage.[26] We find some further specific instructions on the form of the celebration of marriage immediately afterwards, in canon 781: 'If at any time the church has to judge the validity of the marriage of non-baptized Catholics: 1. Concerning the law by which the parties were bound at the time of the celebration of the marriage, canon 780§2 shall be observed; 2. As for the form of the celebration of marriage, the church recognizes every form prescribed or allowed by the law to which the parties were subject at the time of the celebration of the marriage, provided that the consent has been expressed publicly and that if at least one party is a faithful Christian of a non-Catholic Eastern church the marriage has been celebrated in a sacred rite.' Here the issue is not a mixed marriage, as in the previous canon, but a marriage between non-Catholic spouses.

The text gives indications to ecclesiastical tribunals which can be called to judge these marriages. First of all it refers to the law which applies to the non-Catholic spouse at the time of the celebration of the marriage; then specific remarks are made about the form of the celebration. While respecting the law of each party, the Catholic church requires at least a public form of matrimonial consent. Moreover a further demand is added for marriages in which one of the spouses belongs to a non-Catholic Eastern church at the moment of the celebration, as in this case the marriage must have been celebrated in a sacred rite. In other words, there must be at least a priest to confer the blessing. The Catholic church here takes into account the importance of this rite in the non-Catholic Eastern churches for the validity of marriages.

Esteem for the non-Catholic churches and ecclesial communities is manifested in a desire to respect their own character and in particular their right to govern themselves in accordance with their own disciplines and in harmony with the decree *Unitatis redintegratio*.[27]

III. Some forms of contact and collaboration

Two types of institution in the Eastern Catholic churches make it possible explicitly to issue invitations to members belonging to non-Catholic churches or ecclesial communities. These are the patriarchal assembly, a consultative council of the whole of the patriarchal church, and the eparchial assembly.[28] However, it is pointed out that those invited have only the status of 'observers', though this does not prevent the statutes of these assemblies allowing them to participate actively in debates.

The participation of hierarchs of churches which are not yet in full communion with the Catholic churches must be approved of by the statutes of each assembly of the hierarchs of several churches with their own law.[29]

A form of real collaboration is proposed for translations of the Bible: 'Access to Holy Scripture must be broadly open to the Christian faithful; that is why, where they are lacking, appropriate and correct translations with sufficient explanations must be made under the auspices of the eparchial bishops, and even, to the degree that that can be done in a convenient and useful way, in collaboration with other Christians.'[30]

IV. Sharing in divine worship and sacramental life[31]

The new canon law, both that of CIC and CCEO, contains new stipulations relating to ecumenical advances over the sacraments. Thus canon 844 of CIC has an equivalent in canon 671 of CCEO, the two being guided by the conviction that the sacraments are not means for re-establishing Christian unity but are rather signs of the reality of the unity of faith, worship and sacramental life in the Christian community. At the same time, through baptism, the members of other churches and ecclesial communities are in a real, albeit imperfect, communion with the Catholic church.[32] These two basic principles explain access to the sacraments of the Catholic church and the restrictions in this domain. In canon 671, it is provided that Catholic faithful who physically or morally have no access to a Catholic minister can in certain conditions receive some of the sacraments, namely those of penitence, the eucharist and the anointing of the sick, from non-Catholic ministers, provided that the sacraments are valid in these churches. Moreover there has to be a spiritual necessity or utility, and the danger of error or indifference has to be avoided.[33] On the other hand, where non-Catholic faithful want to receive the sacraments from the hands of Catholic ministers, a distinction is made depending on the church or ecclesial community to which they belong.

As a result, Catholic ministers can legitimately administer the sacraments mentioned above to the faithful of the non-Catholic Eastern churches, provided that these ask for them of their own free will and are of a due disposition.[34] The same approach can be taken to the faithful of other churches who according to the judgment of the Holy See are in the same condition as the non-Catholic Eastern churches. But if the faithful belong to ecclesial communities, it is necessary not only for them to make the request of their own free will and to be of a due disposition, but also to show towards these sacraments a faith in conformity with the Catholic faith. Moreover in the judgment of the eparchial bishop or the synod of bishops of the patriarchal church (or archiepiscopal major church) or the council of the hierarchy of the metropolitan church with its own law, there must be danger of death or some other grave necessity. We can note in these texts a kind of gradation depending on whether the church or ecclesial community is close to the Catholic church in its faith or not. The closest are the Eastern non-Catholic churches, then other churches – it remains to be seen which – and finally the ecclesial communities.[35]

In connection with these last a difference between the CIC and CCEO needs to be indicated. The CIC requires that these faithful 'show Catholic faith over these sacraments',[36] whereas the CCEO speaks in this connection of a faith 'in conformity with the faith of the Catholic church'.[37] This last formulation is more in conformity with Vatican II and makes it easier to distinguish between the faith and its expression.[38] On the other hand, we note a desire to avoid any form of proselytism, given that it is required that non-Catholic faithful should ask for these sacraments on their own initiative.

To conclude this canon 671, if there were a desire to issue norms of particular law on the situations mentioned above, it would be necessary to consult the competent authority, at least the local authority, of the church or non-Catholic ecclesial community concerned.[39] Here the Catholic hierarch of the place is envisaged.[40]

Some other norms of CCEO may be added to these general rules for sharing sacramental life. Thus on the subject of the eucharist it is prescribed that a priest needs the permission of the hierarch of a place to celebrate the divine liturgy in a church of non-Catholics.[41] Here the hierarch of the Catholic place is envisaged.[42]

Several norms relating to baptism have found a place in CCEO. A Catholic minister may legitimately baptize a child of non-Catholic parents if there is 'such danger to its life that one can foresee its death before it attains the age of reason'.[43] Apart from such a danger of death, the child of non-Catholic Christians is legitimately baptized if one of the parents or both together or its guardian call for this and it is physically or morally impossible for them to have access to their own minister.[44] For good reason it is possible to accept as a sponsor at baptism a Christian faithful from a non-Catholic Eastern church, but together with a Catholic sponsor.[45] This condition is explained by the fact that to be a sponsor means not only to bring up the child in the Catholic faith but also to be a representative of the community of faith,[46] something which cannot be asked of a non-Catholic sponsor.

Special attention is also paid to marriage in the Eastern canon law. Mixed marriages, i.e. marriages between a Catholic party and a non-Catholic party, no longer constitute an impediment to the legitimacy of the marriage, but from now on require permission from the competent authority.[47] In that case the non-Catholic party will be informed by the promises made by the Catholic party, namely to remove the dangers of abandoning the faith and do everything possible to baptize and bring up the children in the Catholic church.[48] An instruction follows on the ends and essential properties of marriage, namely the well-being of the spouses and the procreation and education of children, together with the unity and indissolubility of marriage. The future spouses must not exclude one or more of these essential ends and properties.[49]

In the celebration of these marriages, an exception is made to the principle that a member of the Catholic church, to celebrate a valid marriage, has to respect the form of celebration of the marriage prescribed by canon law, for in the case of a marriage between a Catholic party and a Christian party belonging to a non-Catholic Eastern church this form relates only to the legitimacy of the marriage, provided that the blessing of a priest is required for its validity, 'observing the other prescriptions of the law'.[50] This last clause is somewhat enigmatic. Canonical doctrine has to elaborate precisely what is meant by these other legal prescriptions. After the marriage the hierarchs of the place and the other pastors of souls will help the spouses to encourage the unity of communion of conjugal and family life.[51]

On the other hand, Catholics who are led to be married only before witnesses, because of the impossibility of finding a competent priest, a form of marriage called 'extraordinary', can appeal to another priest, even is he is not a Catholic, to bless their marriage.[52] Conversely, a Catholic priest could, with the authorization of the hierarch of the place, bless the marriage of faithful Christians of a non-Catholic Eastern church if these found it impossible, without serious inconvenience, to find a priest of their church, and provided that they asked for this spontaneously and that nothing contravened the valid or legitimate celebration of the marriage. In that case the Catholic priest must immediately inform the competent authority of these faithful before blessing the marriage.[53] The *raison d'être* of this norm, like that of the previous one, lies in the fundamental right, accorded to every human being, to be able to marry. Here the Catholic church wants to come to the help of non-Catholic Eastern faithful so that they can realize this right. However, it remains to be seen whether this type of marriage will be recognized as valid in the church of the couple concerned.

Over and above these rules on the sharing of sacramental life, CCEO also contains a norm which is aimed at divine worship in its broader sense and which has no equivalent in CIC, namely that the Catholic faithful can be present at the divine worship of other Christians and take part in it, 'observing what has been decided by the eparchial bishop or the superior authority, and taking account of the degree of communion with the Catholic church'.[54]

The eparchial bishop could thus make a Catholic building, a cemetery or a church available to non-Catholic Christians who had no place to celebrate divine worship, depending on the particular law of his church with its own law.[55]

Among the sacred signs called sacramentals, ecclesiastical funerals can also be given to baptized non-Catholics, unless it was clear that the dead person did not want such a funeral, again according to the wise judgment of the hierarch of the place and provided that the persons's own minister was not available.[56]

Conclusion

The CCEO tries to promote ecumenism in a general way by designating organisms at different levels of the church which must be specially concerned with it, and persons by virtue of their functions. The attitude towards the churches and ecclesial communities which are not in full communion with the Catholic church bears witness to an attitude of respect, notably a concern to avoid all proselytism, and it even recognizes their own law, above all in the Catholic matrimonial sphere. On the other hand, respect for their own disciplines leads CCEO equally to give them the right to receive the sacraments from their own ministers in Catholic institutions.

Furthermore, in the framework of the Catholic church, non-Catholic baptized can be observers at certain assemblies; their ecclesiastical authorities have to be consulted and will collaborate, especially in the assemblies of hierarchs, over translations of the Bible and in developing a particular law for sharing sacramental life.

Sharing divine worship and sacramental law is allowed, but always respecting several conditions and taking account of the different degrees of communion with each non-Catholic church or ecclesial communion in particular.

It is understandable that CCEO pays special attention to the non-Catholic Eastern churches by virtue of their proximity in matters of discipline to the

Eastern Catholic churches. All in all, Eastern canon law has made real progress by comparison with previous law. However, in general canon law reflects the reality of things without being able to move ahead of them (*ius sequitur vitam*). Much will depend on the attention paid to the breath of the Spirit.

Translated by John Bowden

Notes

1. What is important here is the relationship between the church of Christ and the Catholic church, which is expressed not only by the verb *est*, which would denote an identification between the two, but by the verb *subsistit in*, suggesting that at least some elements of the church of Christ can (also) be found outside the Catholic church.

2. In this article, as requested, I shall limit myself to the Code. The space allotted allows reference to the ecumenical Directory, approved on 25 March 1994, only on exceptional occasions. Besides, this document is not typical of the Eastern Catholic churches, since it also applies to the Latin church.

3. Cf. *Nuntia* 3, 1976, p.20, for the English text. This specific mission of the Eastern Catholic churches already figured in the decree *Orientalium Ecclesiarum* no.24, indicating as concrete means prayer, exemplary living, faithfulness to the ancient Eastern traditions, a better mutual knowledge and fraternal collaboration and esteem of things and people.

4. Ibid.

5. Cf. *Code of Canons of the Eastern Churches*, Canon Law Society of America 1992. [Translator's note: unfortunately, I have been unable to locate a copy of this text within the time available. The translations given here are therefore my own.]

6. *AAS* 83, 1991, no. 6, p. 493.

7. Unlike CIC, CCEO is not organized in books but under titles, which are themselves divided into chapters.

8. Canon 902. By comparison with c. 755§1 of CIC note that this attributes the encouragement and direction of the ecumenical movement mainly to the college of bishops and the Holy See, then to the bishops and conferences of bishops without speaking of the other faithful. The title in question contains canons 902–908.

9. Notably the text of *Orientalium Ecclesiarum* no. 24, see n. 3 above.

10. Cf. c. 905. But this caution is not new.

11. Cf. c. 27. All the Eastern churches recognized by the supreme authority of the church, and also the Latin church, are considered as 'churches with their own law', which is a common denominator. Then each church is given its own status depending on whether it is (in descending order of 'autonomy' from Rome) a patriarchal church, a major archiepiscopal church (assimilated in almost every

respect to a patriarchal church, cf. c.152), a metropolitan church with its own law, or another with a hierarchy at its head and depending immediately on the Holy See.

12. C. 904, §§1 and 2.
13. C. 904, §3.
14. C. 906.
15. C. 908. We shall return later to communication in sacred things.
16. Cf. c.192§2. Curiously, we do not find here an equivalent of c.383§ 3 of CIC, which not only speaks of encouraging ecumenism but also wants the diocesan bishop to behave with generosity and charity towards brothers who are not in full communion with the Catholic church.
17. C. 293.
18. Cf. c. 360§4: 'As long as the unity willed by Christ for his church is not fully realized, ecumenism will be one of the necessary aspects of any theological discipline.' This text emphasizes the fact that the re-establishment of unity is an obligation of divine right, since it is 'willed by Christ'. We also find it in c. 902, which mentions 'the full unity of the church desired by the Lord'. Then c. 352§3 prescribes that seminarians shall be instructed, among other things, in the needs of the apostolate of ecumenism.
19. Cf. c. 625: 'Catechesis must have an ecumenical dimension in giving a correct image of the other churches and ecclesial communities', followed by a caution: 'however, it is important to see that the correct perspective of Catholic catechesis is given in all certainty'. This warning seems to want to avoid a kind of syncretism. However, in my view it would seem superfluous, because the correct image of the other churches and ecclesial communities implies that the differences from the Catholic church and its faith are brought out. On the other hand, the apostolic adhortation *Catechesi tradendae* of 16 October, the source of this canon, does not mention this caution in paragraphs 32 and 33, which serve as the basis for the text. On the contrary, we read that a correct and loyal presentation of the other churches and ecclesial communities 'will help Catholics on the one hand to deepen their faith and on the other better to know and esteem their other Christian brothers, thus facilitating the common quest for the way towards full unity in the whole truth'.
20. Cf. c. 907.
21. Cf. c. 634§ 2.
22. One could almost say that canon 907, which moreover does not have its equivalent in the CIC, extends to other Christians in a particular context relating to the Catholic church the fundamental right of the Catholic faithful to receive from the pastors of the church the help which comes from the spiritual goods of the church, above all the word of God and the sacraments (cf. CCEO c.16).
23. Cf. for example cc. 332§ 4 and 671§§3,4. It should be noted that CIC speaks of 'communities', omitting the adjective 'ecclesial', which moreover was only added at a late stage to c.671 of CCEO. Cf. *Nuntia* 27, 1988, 56, 83. Cf. also

Myriam Wijlens, *Sharing the Eucharist. A Theological Evaluation of the Post Conciliar Legislation*, Lanham, New York and Oxford 2000, pp.298, 328.

24. Canon 1: 'The canons of the present Code relate to all the Eastern Catholic churches and *to them alone*' (my italics).

25. Cf. c.1490: 'Those who have been baptized *in the Catholic church* or those who have been received there are bound by the purely ecclesiastical laws . . .' (my italics). The preceding law would make these ecclesiastical laws obligatory for all the baptized, whether Catholic or not. The divine law is another matter.

26. D. Salachas, 'Il nuovo Codice dei Canoni delle Chiese Orientali. Prospettive ecumeniche e limiti', *Euntes Docete* 49, 1996, pp.251–2.

27. Cf. no.16 of this decree. As another example of respect one could read cc. 896–7 and also 901, on the subject of non-Catholic baptized who want to have full communion with the Catholic church. What would be required of them would only be what is necessary – more precisely, for the Christians of an Eastern Catholic church only the profession of the Catholic faith – whereas adaptations of this demand would have to be made for other non-Catholic Christians who did not belong to a non-Catholic Eastern church. I shall not speak of the reception of these non-Catholic faithful, since this is not the topic at issue.

28. Cf. c. 143§4: 'Some observers belonging to non-Catholic churches or ecclesial communities can also be invited to the patriarchal assembly.' The same terms are used in c. 238§3 in connection with the eparchial assembly. This is comparable to a diocesan synod, 'eparchy' being the equivalent term to diocese. So one could even compare the patriarchal assembly with this kind of gathering, making it clear that it involves not only an eparchy but a whole major Eastern, patriarchal or archiepiscopal church.

29. Cf. c. 322§4. 'Hierarchs' is equivalent to the Latin term 'ordinaries'. The fact that these types of assembly bring together ecclesiastical authorities from several Eastern Catholic churches exercising their power in the same nation or region with a view to a better collaboration, without imposing the decisions of each of them, explains this extension to non-Catholic authorities in the same region, since in the East there is often such a 'concentration' of ecclesiastical authorities.

30. Cf. c. 655§1.

31. This latter is generally designated by the Latin term *communicatio in sacris*.

32. Directory, no.129.

33. Cf. c. 671§2. This is about the reception of the sacraments in a non-Catholic Eastern church. The Directory obliges Catholics to respect as far as possible the Eastern discipline on the sacraments.

34. In this connection we find in Directory no.125 the same obligation to respect the particular discipline of these faithful, and to avoid any kind of proselytism, even in appearance.

35. Cf. *Unitatis Redintegratio* 14–18 and 21–23.

36. CIC c. 844§4: '*dummodo quoad eadem sacramenta fidem catholicam manifestent*'.

37. CCEO c. 671§4: '*dummodo circa eadem sacramenta fidem manifestent fidei Ecclesiae catholicae* consentaneam' (my emphasis).

38. Wijlens, *Sharing the Eucharist* (n. 23), p.330.

39. CCEO c. 671§5; CIC c. 844§5 contains the same norm except that it mentions the competent Catholic authorities, namely the diocesan bishop and the conference of bishops. The different organization of the Eastern Catholic churches means that the authorities competent to administer a particular law are in fact the eparchial bishop and the synod of bishops of the major patriarchal or archiepiscopal churches and the council of the hierarchs of the metropolitan church with its own law – in other words the highest authorities at the level of each church with its own law.

40. Cf. D. Salachas, *Teologia e disciplina dei sacramenti nei Codici latino e orientale. Studio teologico-giuridico comparativo*, Bologna 1999, 198.

41. Cf. c. 705§2.

42. Salachas, *Teologia e disciplina dei sacramenti nei Codici latino e orientale* (n. 40), p.198.

43. Cf. c. 681§4.

44. C. 685§5.

45. C. 685§3.

46. See Directory, no. 98.

47. Cf. c. 813. Cf. the legal precedent in the *motu proprio Crebrae Allatae*, promulgated on 22 February 1949, cc. 50–51.

48. By way of comparison, in canon 52 *Crebrae allatae* would oblige the Catholic partner to work towards the conversion of his or her non-Catholic spouse.

49. C. 814§§1–3.

50. C. 834§2.

51. Cf. c. 816.

52. See c. 832§2.

53. C. 833.

54. Cf. c. 670§1.

55. C. 670§2.

56. Cf. c. 876.1.

Patterns of Synodality Today

PIERRE VALLIN

There are considerable difficulties in the way of presenting an overall picture of synodal institutions in the present Christian world. On the one hand, there are institutions that bear a title derived from the Greek notion of synod. But they vary greatly among themselves. On the other hand, some institutions carry out the work programme suggested by the concept: they meet in order to achieve a common consensus, but they are not called synods. We should therefore look to a typology going across the actual vocabulary, using criteria drawn from the practice of 'concerting'. This is what I shall attempt here. The construction has a descriptive purpose, but the image thus presented of the notion of 'synodality' raises questions concerning the possible evaluation, within the Christian tradition, of the practices evoked and their lasting relevance. I shall return to this latter aspect by way of conclusion.

For now, let us tackle the description by evoking the origins of the usage of the notion of synod in Christian history, particularly in the East.

I. Origins of the vocabulary

The word 'synod' refers back culturally to Christian traditions – to the Christian movement, one might even say, in the variety of the forms it has taken from its origins with the followers of Jesus Christ.[1] In the very extensive diversity of social forms springing from the bosom of this historical movement, the name 'synod' relates to its oldest usage in the life of the Christian communities. This usage seems to have originated around the end of the second century, in the Christian world where Greek was the main language. It most likely referred then to local gatherings made up of representatives of several churches, with a mainly doctrinal function – to react against errors seen as threatening and to decide what disciplinary measures needed to be taken in a region where these difficulties arose.[2] In synodal gatherings, then, the role of 'intendants' or bishops came to be defined, a role that was to become increasingly important in the churches. It is, however, likely that arrangements the Latin communities in Africa considered normal became fairly generalized: councils were held in the presence of the people.[3]

It should be stressed that the authority of the synod, at this initial stage, was that of the gathering itself, where the presence of the Lord, of his Spirit, was judged to be manifest. At the same time, this authority was not perceived in an isolated fashion, attached to a measure, to a formula. The acceptance of the authority of this synodal event referred it to the whole made up of the scriptures and their interpretation in the life of the churches. As a result, acceptance was not devoid of some distancing, which could lead to revision on certain points, as circumstances dictated. One synodal authority could interpret what had gone before it.[4]

With local variations, which were undoubtedly important, a synodal institution of this type would have developed in the churches in the eastern part of the Roman Empire, and it still remains characteristic of these churches today.[5] Two main changes took place. The first consisted in defining territory, marked out in permanent fashion after the model of the imperial province or region. Within this framework synods met regularly, with all the bishops within its boundaries either present or represented. The second characteristic to evolve was that the synod was presided over by the titular of the metropolitan see, for a province, or by that of the patriarchal see, for a more extensive region (with some churches becoming autocephalous). It is notable that Cyprian refused a higher authority for himself, despite being called on to preside at the council for Christian Africa.[6]

Constantinople was the main focus of the institution of a permanent synod, formed around the president by suffragan bishops from nearby sees and bishops temporarily resident in the city at the principal see. A comparable body formed around the Bishop of Rome.

Even if the authority of the bishops was in evidence at synods, these assemblies continued to benefit from a lay presence, thereby to an extent being able to ensure that the faithful people took part. These were often delegates or people who held public office. To varying extents, one can speak of mixed synods, but the predominance – in principle – of episcopal authority was often forcefully asserted. The same held true for the local, provincial, or sometimes national (in the broad mediaeval sense) councils held in the West. But with these Western councils, the determination was voiced to place the decisions made by local assemblies under the authority of the Roman See, which was opposed on principle – though not always in practice – to the influence of lay lords or that of secular urban authorities.

II. From the origins of the term to a general notion

Should we give the first sense in which the term synod (or *concilium* in Latin) was used the overall interpretation this article is supposed to propose? We need to keep the distinction between the idea of a synod that supposes the presence of lay faithful and the later tendency to use the concept for bodies relying mainly on episcopal authority. In the second type there is a co-ordinating role, to be exercised in relation to all the churches within the jurisdiction of the synod, reserved to a *protos*, in the word used by the Greeks, in other words to the titular of the principal see of the territory or jurisdiction concerned, the metropolitan or patriarchal see.

There was certainly a link between the synodal institution devised by the churches and the sort of deliberative assemblies familiar in the world of classical Antiquity – and then in the Middle Ages in the West. One then raise a question about communities that developed – or were to arise later – in cultures in which the custom of collective deliberation on the Western model is not found: one, that is, with a statutary function, that meets regularly, and which expects to base its decisions on issues determined by a majority voice. Do such cases exist? The possibility of them can remain in a hypothetical manner; we then need to wait for original autonomous bodies to emerge.

The question raised has a further immediate relevance. How far should we link the idea of synodality to that of episcopacy? The ground can partly be cleared, or at least have paths drawn across it, by evoking two other concepts: those of conciliarity and collegiality.

Historically, the idea of conciliarity has been in relation or tension with that of primacy, of papacy, and so in the line of a tradition concerning the exercise of ecclesial jurisdiction, of powers of directing and teaching, that touches a large proportion of Christian churches.[7] The tendency of 'conciliarism' is then to oppose episcopal authority, and especially its crown, the pontifical primacy, with the authority of the Christian people as a whole, so that the intervention of political or theological leaders of this faithful people would then have a greater role. This form of 'synodality' does not appear to correspond to the current model.

III. The question of 'Councils of Churches'

We can now turn to another reality, which is certainly current, the development of ideas of 'council' in the ecumenical context. The English word 'council' has become widely used (here translating French *conseil* and

German *Rat*) for institutions that act across the boundaries of otherwise still separate churches.[8] Such institutions can also go by other names, especially that of 'conference', as in the 'Conference of European Churches'. These are bodies that bring several churches together, either acting as their instrument in particular tasks or as 'provisional' places for expressing the common search for church unity. Generally Protestant in origin, these councils – such as the World Council of Churches itself – can by now involve church communities attached to Orthodoxy, to non-Chalcedonian churches, or to Roman Catholicism, especially where collaboration on a local, regional, or national level is at issue.

I should say that, at least on the descriptive level, these 'councils' can be described as being an exercise of 'synodality' in the sense put forward here, that of a descriptive concept, working nonetheless for more general reflection of an ecclesiological nature. It is clear that such unions cannot execute significant actions unless they receive approval from the episcopal authorities – in cases, that is, where the churches participating in these joint bodies, or at least some of them, have a hierarchical structure. Nevertheless, one can – in my view – state that the representation then operating is less properly 'episcopal' or 'collegial' (I shall come back to this notion later) than 'synodal'. By this I mean that representation is made up of a specific church group, including lay people, consisting either of specialists or experts, or of militants and practitioners supporting joint actions, or of lay people who share in the ministry of celebrating ecumenical liturgies.

We can reckon that the synodality in question here will arise first as an internal process in each of the churches concerned; it is on this basis that these will become involved, when representatives they send come together in 'councils' or 'conferences'. These are representatives who can be defined in ecclesiological terms as the specific artisans of a synodal consensus, first within their own church grouping and then once the aim of their work and liturgies has become that of taking part in gatherings involving other church groups.[9]

These 'councils of churches' have their counterpart in the regional assemblies promoted under various circumstances by the Catholic churches *sui juris*, those that can be grouped under the heading of Uniate churches. It is possible, though, that these assemblies have sometimes remained at the level of inter-episcopal consultations, with relatively little participation by ordinary priests or lay people.

IV. The question of episcopal collegiality

The idea of 'collegiality' – whatever the origin of its current Catholic usage as sanctioned by Vatican II may be – requires one to think of a 'college', made up of members juridically equal in status, distinguished from the body of the faithful, and equally distinguished from those holding various responsibilities in the life of the church who are not qualified for this collegial position. This idea is linked to current Catholic theology of the episcopate and to the role played within this body by the Bishop of Rome. This sort of polarization of the concept around the hierarchical order of the episcopate today sometimes leads theologians and canonists to distinguish between those institutions that develop an ecclesial dimension of collegiality and those in which the body of the faithful, or at least 'the greater part of the people – in the above-quoted expression from a council of Carthage – effectively participate, statutorily planned and codified. A very clear case of the second type in the Catholic Church, according to the 1983 Code of Canon Law, is that of special councils – provincial or plenary (the latter corresponding to the jurisdiction of a Bishops' Conference) – in which a sharing by various active ministries in the dioceses concerned is foreseen: priests and deacons, religious, lay people in various situations or with pastoral responsibilities.

On the other hand, this participation is not statutory in Bishops' Conferences, even if something of the sort can be introduced as occasion demands, with a limited consultative function. Clearly, having distinguished these two aspects and the institutions that correspond most closely to each of them, we need next to see how they relate to one another.[10]

It is true that we now have, in the play between equal bishops and the primacy – so in full 'episcopality' – the Roman institution of the 'synod of bishops', which in its origin, announced by Paul VI at the opening of the fourth session of Vatican II, on 15 September 1965, would seem to bear some relationship to the conciliar affirmation of 'collegiality'.[11] The evolution of this institution cannot be traced here. One important aspect has been the transition, under the present pontificate, to continental synods, which have occasioned lively participation, at the preparation stages above all, by active groups in the individual churches, in dioceses, movements, religious congregations. For various reasons, the part played by the Bishop of Rome in convoking these various general or continental synods has been decisive. Their scope and structure have been the subject of some debate.

From the viewpoint followed here, it is important not to neglect the importance of the wider consultative gatherings these episcopal synods have

brought about, first through the planned meeting, then from its pro-
longations as they have occurred.

V. Diocesan synods and Bishops' Conferences

The link with the episcopate is clear in the case of the other Roman Catholic
institution derived from Vatican II that has been called 'synod': the diocesan
synod. The part played by the local bishop is crucial here, in deciding
whether to hold a synod, in establishing its *modus operandi*, and in the way its
results are implemented.[12] At the same time, the proper nature of such an
institution, as it has been incorporated in the 1983 Code of Canon Law
(applicable in the first place to the Latin church), is to mix the bishop's
initiative with a broad participation of priests, of religious, of actively committed lay people, and of 'simple faithful' not holding any defined pastoral
responsibilities.

As a working hypothesis, we can say that here we have a decisive element
that allows us to fashion an operational idea of the notion of synodality,
beyond its simple designation by the original Greek word. The reference to
episcopal collegiality would be one dimension of it,[13] but in a position of
tension or complementarity with regard to the element of community
participation open to the various groups who make up the life of a local or
particular church.

Within this perspective, participation by priests, deacons, religious,
and lay people in the various diocesan councils envisaged by the Code or
introduced locally by custom can also be called 'synodal'. These councils can
also quite often have a place in inter-diocesan consultations.[14]

In the realm of synodality, the diocesan council has its counterpart,
juridically more precisely structured on this point of participation by the
faithful, in the present canonical institution of special (regional or provincial) councils already briefly referred to. But their juridical possibilities have
remained marginal, as in practice they have not recently been called on.

Within the descriptive hypothesis put forward here, the Bishops'
Conferences would be an example of episcopal exercise of collegiality. This
opinion would appear to be confirmed by the fact that the current rules of
Latin canon law make it possible for certain bishops who are legitimately
consecrated but not currently titulars of a see to be members of a Conference. Nevertheless, it is clear that the bishop, in the Commissions and
Assemblies, represents his church – using the word in the broad sense, with
'church' meaning all the faithful who look to him, even if they are not under
his direct jurisdiction. It is important to remember that the purpose of the

present argument is not to deny Bishops' Conferences – linked to the exercise of collegiality by legitimately ordained bishops – a real synodality, in the form of participation by the local churches represented at them. They are genuinely synodal through their bishops, but they are equally so by the fact of the involvement, present or future, of their resources, of their various active bodies, in the actions envisaged by inter-episcopal consultations. This involvement clearly needs to be made the subject of a fairly precise examination from a juridical standpoint.[15]

One particular problem we can look at now is that of trials or experiences of synods, with wide participation by priests and lay people, organized on a national scale, covering the jurisdiction of a Bishops' Conference. The most prominent example of this to date is the common synod of German dioceses in the 1970s. This produced a number of tensions on the level of how to treat the possibility of collective stances taken and whether or not to combine the local churches involved.[16]

This is in line with a general problem for synods – paralleling that raised by the effective sidelining of the canonical conditions for holding local, regional, and national synods. Diocesan synods do actually meet together, and this can produce a lively shared reflection. But the decisions taken often tend to be very limited in their scope compared to the gravity of the problems aired. Why go to so much trouble? As a canonist has remarked, any synod that has succeeded has in fact been experienced as a 'happening'. That supposes a *kairos*, a favourable moment, and this is not something that can be manufactured at will.[17]

Another aspect of sharing in church government involves base communities and movements, as well as – still predominantly, no doubt – parish life and the various ways parishes are structured. There has been a widespread effort made to promote the involvement of lay people in leadership of their communities, but results have not always been convincing, at least among the tired Christian peoples of Western societies. A report prepared on French-speaking parishes in the Reformed tradition, nevertheless, is clear and far from pessimistic.[18]

VI. Synodal organization of the Reformed churches

Let us now take a brief look at synods that have an institutional place in the churches of the Protestant tradition.[19] In churches deriving from Luther, the institution, after several early trials – and not without some tension with Geneva – was endorsed by a synod held in Poitiers in 1557, followed by a national one in Paris in 1559.[20] The Confession of Faith known as that of

La Rochelle, also in 1559, strongly asserted the autonomy of each pastor together with his local community and not till its article 32 did it add that it is good and useful for pastors to 'consider among themselves the means they might take for the health of the whole body', and also that it is good for there to be 'some special provisions for each place'. It would seem that this article did not go so far as to sanction as such the institution of a pyramidal synodal system, starting from the local base and working up to the national level, but it was moving in that direction. This is in any case what later emerged in the churches produced by Calvin's Reformation and, through imitation or borrowing, in those of Lutheran origin that adopted comparable institutions.

In Protestant churches, the membership of the synodal body is based, according to varying rules, on representation of the different members of the local church: pastors, elders, plain faithful. There is provision for a president of the synod, but most Reformed churches would not see this as implying recognition that the president exercises any personal power that could be called episcopal in nature.

Synods are normally seen as sharing in responsibility for doctrinal matters, but many Reformed communities allow for wide discretion in this domain, which can appear to contrast with the demanding rigour their synodal bodies bring to respect for fixed canonical procedures on questions of discipline, organization, and elections to office. The lack of a higher pastoral authority – that of an Eastern- or Roman-style bishop – makes it necessary to have a synodal structure like this, more clearly regulated by custom and rule and often under lay supervision. On the other hand, the scope offered for reflection on doctrinal matters tends to mean that pastors have the greater say.

From a general theological point of view, one can say that actual guidance by the prophetic Spirit is usually referred in Reformed Protestant culture to the local community (at parish or congregation level) rather than to synodal assemblies. The church ministry of the latter is seen more as an aid – limited and circumstantial – of an advisory nature, not as a charismatic event to be taken on trust.

This strongly external conception helps to explain the place often taken in Protestant tradition and current practice by another form of church gathering. Synodal terminology is not usually employed here, but despite that a certain type of synodal process can be seen at work in it. I am referring to renewal movements, with the part played in them by assemblies on a wider plane than that of the local communities affected by the movement. Such movements do not always arouse the enthusiasm of the traditional churches, but these generally at least stop short of remorselessly sidelining renewals.

Conclusion: Opening out

The scene we have surveyed is too diverse to lead to any simple conclusion. The success of a synod has more of event than of institution about it. As for the institution, it fits into the diversity of juridical rulings the churches apply to themselves, depending on historical, cultural, and theological factors. This diversity is an essential feature. I am going to suggest what might serve as a general guideline to the function of images or models of unity in church life.

A dominant image is inspired by the relationship of husbands to wives in the Letter to the Ephesians. For a church to be one, it has to have a 'single' head. The image used as a guide to understanding Christ's representation to his church is that of the eminence of an individual person. This, however, does not have to be the case, though we can, of course, stay with an ecclesiology by which Christ's authority over his church is represented by ministers, by apostolic authorities – sacramentally, according to patristic theologies.

The analogy with the group of Twelve is relevant, but the image of a college, as suggested by the narrative construction of Acts, can be pushed into the background. The whole question of the ways Christ is represented to the church and to the way this is ordered effectively sends us back to a reading of scripture.[21] This representation of the risen Lord among us here on earth is made into a conceptual and symbolic construction in the Letter to the Ephesians, but it is – decisively from our point of view here – a way of representation that rests on its being exercised through a plurality of different functions and, for each of these ministries, by bringing a plurality of empowered persons into play.[22]

The synodal practice of the churches should bear a close resemblance to the primary structure of church life as such: the coming together of all the baptized, in the unity of the Spirit, for a sharing of all the gifts and charisms. Utopia, of course, but one that has inspired the participation of the faithful in the synodal process. This brings us back to the essentials, those mooted by Paul himself, especially in the letters to the Corinthians and the Romans. But when we come to this general sharing, we come up against the major problem of numbers: there are simply too many for a direct verbal exchange to be possible. We have to move to other levels of 'synodality', bringing 'representatives' into play. Of course this procedure will always be seen as ambiguous. We have to make do with it, however, in the hope that the ministers of this restricted sharing will be authentic 'gifts' of the risen Lord.

Consideration of the need for and difficulties of sharing gifts and charisms in an assembly of shifting size brings us back to the requirement felt by the early church to form synods. The situation has, though, changed considerably since then, as the multiplication of synodal forms we have considered shows. This means that we have to give full consideration to a plurality of synodal forms, each of which has different structures within itself by virtue of its internal composition, and this will affect many people. The central pivot of community exchanges then takes the form of a 'synod', varying in size, made up of a nucleus of representatives, responsible for or benefiting from ecclesial services and charisms, and evidently including those who bear the gift of presidency. There is then a vital appreciation – at least as a play on words of hope – that a concord is being reached, through complex synodalities that can support each other, right up to the widest forms of inter-church exchange.

Translated by Paul Burns

Notes

1. On the concept of 'movement' in the history of Christian groups, see my article 'La fin, le religieux, le politique. Analyses sociales des phénomènes de messianisme', *RSR* 84 (1996), pp.43–66.

2. V. Saxer, 'Le développement des Conciles' (to 300) in *Histoire du christianisme*, 2, Paris 1995, pp.63–8.

3. '*Praesente etiam plebis maxima parte . . .*', prologue to *Sententiae episcoporum* of the council of 256, in Works of Cyprian (G. Hartel), *CSEL*, 3/1, p.435, cited by Saxer in *Historire du christianisme*, 1, Paris 2000, p.803.

4. I have used the major research by H. Ohme, *Kanon Ekklesiastikos. Die Bedeutung des altkirchlichen Kanonbegriffs*, Berlin 1998. The works of H. J. Sieben also throw light on this point.

5. There are several contributions on the Graeco-Eastern tradition in *La Synodalité. La participation an gouvernement de l'Eglise*, 1, Acts of the Seventh International Congress of Canon Law, *L'année canonique*, unnumbered, Paris 1992. Synodal organization, typical of the Graeco-Byzantines, has an equivalent in the non-Chalcedonian churches. The practice of the Uniate communities is similar.

6. Prologue to *Sententiae episcoporum*, in Saxer, p.804.

7. 'Conciliarity' has been used to suggest, like the notion of *sobornost*, a dimension intrinsic to any genuinely Christian people, a conception that can imply a downgrading of hierarchical authorities, including councils and synods. See the

article by Dom E. Lanne in N. Lossky et al., *Dictionary of the Ecumenical Movement*, Geneva 1991, pp.212–13.

8. See in ibid., T. F. Best, 'Councils of Churches: Local, National, Regional'.

9. The problem briefly alluded to here is that of the degree to which those who work in ecumenical relations, who tend to be ordinary priests or lay people, participate – or not – compared to the church hierarchy. They do not, except in particular cases, form a delegation as such. But neither do they bring a purely personal witness that does not involve the church body as a whole. I suggest that we have to think in terms of speaking of a synodal type of authority. This will hardly appeal to Orthodox theologians, who are careful to distinguish between ecumenical activity and the conciliar processes called for by the situation of the churches, principally a pan-Orthodox synod – which would call for very careful preparation.

10. P. Valdrini, in the Conclusions to the Paris Colloquy (n. 5 above), discusses this complex relationship. So 'synodality is unthinkable divorced from the episcopal ministry of which it is an essential dimension': pp.852f. Then, on this basis he adds, 'The diocesan bishop or the head of a local church cannot be detached from the people to whom he belongs' – the people whom he in any case represents. But 'every member . . . has a right to participate', which is not exhausted, one might say, by episcopal mediation. This tension, Valdrini stresses, calls for development of a canonical theory of particpation: p.855.

11. There are numerous works on the origins of the 'Synod of Bishops'. On the institution see G. P. Milano, 'Il sinodo dei Vescovoi: natura, funzioni, rappresentatività', in *La Synodalité* (n. 5 above), 1, pp.167–82. Contributions and arguments in *Paolo VI e la Collegialità episcopale*, Brescia and Rome 1995. Finally, P. Valdrini et al., *Droit Canonique (Précis Dalloz)*, 2d ed., Paris 1999, pp.244ff.

12. See the report (on Italy) by the sociologist S. Abbruzese, 'Centralisation diocésaine et production institutionelle de la participation', in J. Palard (ed), *Le gouvernement de l'Eglise catholique. Synodes et exercice du pouvoir*, Paris 1997, pp.97–112: his thesis is that synods have proved mainly a new way for bishops to exercise personal power.

13. In the 'councils' concerned, churches that do not allow for an episcopal role comparable to that of the bishoprics of East or West have met together. Hypothetically speaking, though, one can call the assemblies of these 'councils of churches' synods to the extent that the church groups who make them up admit – at least jointly or mostly – the legitimacy, not to say significance, of the part played in the gathering envisaged by the 'council' by churches that have an episcopal type of structure. This is a question in need of further theological examination.

14. H. Legrand, 'Synodes et conseils de l'après-concile. Quelques enjeux ecclésiologiques', *NRT* 86 (1976), pp.193–216: written before the 1983 Code, this is still a basic work. For an analysis of the situation in African dioceses see R.

Kulimushi Mutarushawa, *La charge pastorale. Droit universel et droit local*, Paris 1999, pp.296ff.: this work is important for renewal of the 'organic structures of the parish': pp.164ff.

15. G. Feliciani, 'Le Conferenze episcopali como fonte di Diritto particolare', *Folia canonica* 2 (Budapest 1999), pp.21–9, remarks that several recent concordatory documents assign competence for relations with the State to the Bishops' Conference – something that could closely involve the special resources of groups of lay people.

16. B. Franck, *Actualité nouvelle des Synodes: le synod comun des diocèses allemands (1971–1975)*, Paris 1980. See also a report on the German-speaking diocesan synods by W. Schulz in *La Synodalité*, 2, pp.620–49. He points to a feeling of weariness among Catholics, while M. Hebrard, *Révolution tranquille chez les Catholiques. Voyage au pays des synodes diocésains*, Paris 1989, points to mal-functions but is generally optimistic. From the canonical standpoint see J.-C. Durand, 'Les synodes en France. Droit et institution', in *Le gouvernement de l'Eglise*, pp.115–29.

17. According to Schulz, p.649, reporting a colleague.

18. R. J. Campiche et al., *L'exercice du pouvoir dans le Protestantisme. Les conseillers de paroisse de France et de Suisse romane*, Geneva 1990. Compare the reflections of Africa in *La charge pastorale* (n. 14 above).

19. The churches of the Anglican communion have a synodal tradition related to that of the Eastern churches.

20. E. G. Léonard, *Histoire générale du Protestantisme*, 2, Paris 1961, pp.93–103.

21. For a Catholic ecclesiology that puts forward a renewed view of the question of how Christ is represented to his church see J. Werbick, *Kirche. Ein ekklesiologischer Entwurf für Studium und Praxis*, Freiburg 1994 (and see my review in *RSR* 85 [1997], pp.151–3).

22. Eph. 4.1–6. See H. Schlier, *Der Brief an die Epheser*, Düsseldorf 1957, pp.190–209.

The Paradigm of Assisi

FAUSTINO TEIXEIRA

The World Day of Prayer for Peace, held in Assisi in 1986, was a basic land-mark in the field of inter-faith dialogue. For the first time in history, a large number of religious leaders gathered together in order to pray and witness to the transcendental nature of peace. Those who took part in the experience are unanimous in affirming its extraordinary nature. In the view of the Dalai Lama, the meeting at Assisi had extremely beneficient results, since 'it symbolized the solidarity and commitment to peace shown by all those took part in it'.[1] Speaking of the event, Pope John Paul II stated that the un-animity of feeling shown there produced a vibration of 'the deepest strings of the human spirit'.[2] Christians from the various churches and ecclesial communities stood side by side with one another and with representatives of other religious traditions, as companions on the common journey, in a spirit of prayer, fasting, and pilgrimage.

The paradigm of Assisi, which opened up a new horizon of dialogue for the religions, has again become relevant at the present juncture of ecclesial evolution, marked as it is by the complex arguments of the Declaration *Dominus Iesus*, issued by the Congregation for the Doctrine of the Faith in September 2000. This Declaration is in line with a very widespread tendency in the current Catholic religious environment, characterized by affirmation of identity, with an emphasis on the centralization of explicit proclamation. Its publication brought surprise and even consternation to the various bodies working on the question of ecumenism and inter-faith dialogue. A more sober and humble document, one marked with the tone and spirit of the openness of the council, had been hoped for, not one marked with the logic of warnings, typical of those who fail to see the light of mystery shining over near horizons. What was lamented above all was the ignoring of thirty-five years of ecumenical history stamped with the will towards greater communion in diversity. At this time when dialogue is in eclipse, it is opportune and indeed urgent to refresh our memories with the spring-like tonic of that day in Assisi, with all that it brought in the way of challenge and actuality.

I. The singularity of a Spirit event

The importance and novelty of what happened at Assisi was expressed in significant ways both by the participants and by observers and analysts. It did in fact represent a new start and a historical initiative of major importance. Going beyond the intentions of those who took part and breaking out of their empirical envelope, the Assisi event proved to be a 'gesture without precedent', an extraordinary and unique happening that carried an explosive symbolic charge within itself. For Cardinal Willebrands, then president of the Secretariat for Christian Unity, that day at Assisi was 'the most significant ecumenical event since the Second Vatican Council'.[3] The invitation issued by the pope to the leaders of other churches and of the various religious traditions implied an 'act', a 'gesture', that, moving beyond words, would mark a change of outlook on ecumenical relations and on those with the other world religions. It was to be the inauguration of a 'planetary ecumenism', in the phrase coined by the Dominican theologian Marie-Dominique Chenu in his reflection on the event.[4]

The initiative taken at Assisi encouraged not only a creative reception of Vatican II but also the recognition of the value of religions to the world, and it acted as an effective stimulus to reflection on the subject in inter-faith dialogue.[5] In a way not seen before, men and women of different religious traditions came together to witness before the world to the 'transcendent quality of peace'. The very fact the event was convened already showed a unique symbolic meaning, a recognition and acceptance of the legitimacy of other religious traditions in God's saving plan: 'a recognition of these religions and of prayer in particular, a recognition that the religions and prayer not only have a social function but are effective with God'.[6] Not confined to a single act, the Assisi experience had an 'explosive spiritual power', from which 'new peace energies' sprang,[7] with unprecedented repercussions that showed the way forward into new ways of dialogue.

1. The stages of the event

The World Day of Prayer for Peace was prepared some time in advance, with the first official announcement of it made by Pope John Paul II in his closing homily for the Week of Prayer for Christian Unity, on 25 January 1986. The pope spoke of his desire to contribute to the world movement of prayer for peace and announced the idea of a gathering for prayer in the symbolic city of Assisi.[8] Cardinal Roger Etchegaray, president of the *Justitia et Pax* commission, played a major part in the preparations, forming committees to carry out the various tasks. It is worth pointing out that, in the early stages, the work was undertaken by 'minor' bodies in the Roman Curia, in consultation with the pope. The 124 official participants to whom Rome's invitation was sent were made up of sixty-four Christians and sixty-four members of other religious traditions. Of the Christians, twelve were Roman Catholics, while the non-Catholics represented thirteen churches of the Orthodox tradition and a further thirteen from the Reformed families of churches. The religious traditions of Asia had a significant representation, with the Buddhists being the most numerous. Islam's participation was more limited, as was that of Judaism, restricted to a few members of the Jewish community in Rome. Five members of traditional African and American religions were there to represent them.

The principal objective of the day was outlined by Pope John Paul II in his message of welcome, given in Santa Maria dei Angeli on 27 October 1986. It was to be above all 'an eloquent sign of the commitment of all to peace'. The presence of so many religious leaders from all over the world, coming together to pray for peace, was in itself an invitation to a new world awareness, an expression of the attention the religions were paying to the good of humankind. The pope stressed that the proposed initiative did not imply any quest for a religious consensus, any concession to relativism, or negotiation of the convictions of each particular religion, but meant a common search, even in diversity, for deeper spiritual endeavours to bring about true peace. The event was defined as a day of prayer, accompanied by silence, pilgrimage, and fasting.[9]

The course of the day was divided into three specific stages, introduced or concluded with a papal discourse. The first stage was the pope's welcome to those taking part, in the basilica of Santa Maria dei Angeli. Then the various delegations set out in silence for the several places in the mediaeval city designated for the special prayers of each religious tradition. After these special prayers there was a time of pilgrimage, when the participants walked in procession from the different prayer stations to where they were all to meet together. The third and closing act of the day took place in front of the basilica of St Francis. After a brief introduction by Cardinal Etchegaray, the representatives of the different religions present took turns to make their own prayers. The day came to an end with an address by the pope.

2. *Unity in prayer*

One of the most significant aspects of the day was the macro-ecumenical dimension of its prayer. As Claude Geffré has aptly remarked, praying, as a basic attitude of all religious people, 'is more universal than explicit faith in a personalized God. There is a universal language of prayer that transcends the diversity of the religions of the world.'[10] Through prayer, the participants in the gathering were able to express, in different ways, the living presence of an ultimate reality that surpasses all. Through the universal language of prayer, they were all able to have an experience of grace and of sharing. It is true that the organizers were constantly on their guard against any form of religious syncretism, as was shown in the formula chosen for the event: 'together to pray', not 'praying together'. Any kind of common prayer was avoided. At the most delicate stage of the day, when they were all gathered in front of the basilica of St Francis, each particular group came forward out of the common circle in which they were placed in order to pronounce its prayer in a designated space. So the prayers of each group were made one after the other, while the rest remained silent in a posture of respect.[11]

The truth, nevertheless, is that, whatever the intentions of the planners, the scenario bringing all these religious leaders from the various traditions together produced a new sign of the times. This new image broke with the historical burden of centuries of intolerance, of religious struggles, and of ethnic antagonisms. Unity was now being built around prayer for peace, a unity focussed on the horizon of the invisible, on the mystery of otherness, shared by each one of those present. There was an obvious sense of the complexity and tension between the unity of Being and the multiplicity of its representations. The event was a decisive manifestation of respect for otherness. Each tradition was able to express itself in freedom, and all were able to *assist* in sharing the experiences of prayer and of the noblest different ways of entering into relationship with Absolute Being. At one of the most symbolically significant moments, one of the Hindu religious leaders proclaimed the blessing of the Great Spirit over the pope, in recognition of his initiative in bringing them all together for this experience of prayer in Assisi. As the theologian Ernesto Balducci remarked, 'Superstition dared to bless Truth and Truth remained silent in humility! As at the formation of the world, the Spirit with a thousand names hovered over the abyss.'[12]

The simple act of respectfully accompanying someone making his prayer already shows a positive valuation of his religious standing, an opening on to recognition of the special nature of his relationship with God. The gathering at Assisi signified an even greater advance than that expressed by Vatican II in its Declaration on Religious Freedom. The novelty of Assisi emerged in the dynamics of its encounter with the other at the actual moment of his religious experience.[13] This encounter displayed the fact of unity that underlies the diversity of experiences, as the pope himself made clear later:

'On that day, and in the prayer that prompted it and was its only content, it seemed that for a moment the hidden and radical unity that the divine Word [. . .] established among the men and women of the world was also made visible.'[14] As was the recognition that 'all authentic prayer is made under the influence of the Holy Spirit'.[15]

One of the most important documents of the Catholic Church's magisterium on inter-faith dialogue points to the sharing of experiences of prayer and contemplation as the deepest level of forms of dialogue. This is a type of dialogue that provides a 'reciprocal enrichment and fruitful co-operation in promoting and preserving the highest human values and spiritual ideas'.[16] But even at this deep level, we still have to bring out the permanence of differences. What comes about at the level of mystical experience is consciousness of an 'intense companionship', which does not mean it has exhausted the possibility of sharing new and unknown spiritual riches. It is the same God who is experienced, but through diversified experience.[17] Despite all the precautions taken, there can be no denying the presence of mutual communication at this level on that day in Assisi. There was scarcely any tangential contact, but the event in fact provided an existential and spiritual closeness that left its mark those who took part in it.

3. The challenge of peace

One of the basic contributions made by the gathering at Assisi was to indicate the importance of the different religious traditions acting in common to defend and promote human and spiritual values. What was most evident was the absolute need to act for the sake of peace. The meeting of religions took on a very specific significance in this field of ethics, also giving rise to a new 'creaturely communion'. The challenge of peace presents the religions with the imperative of working for the survival of the human race and for a better quality of life for all. The struggle to bring about peace is a challenge facing not just small groups of specialists or strategists; it is a 'universal responsibility'. Religions can here make one of their special contributions. Beyond their differences, this witness for peace is shown to be a 'common basis' of responsibility for solving the most dramatic challenge of our age – 'true peace or catastrophic war'.[18] The overall purpose of the event, emphasized from the start, was to pray for peace, to stress the transcendent value of peace, to harmonize all voices in begging God to grant this essential gift.

II. Fears and reactions provoked

The pioneering nature of the world day of prayer in Assisi did not fail to provoke very definite resistance. There is nothing surprising in the fact that something so novel should provoke uncertainties in various sectors. The previous Code of Canon Law (1917) forbade Catholics to be present at, let alone take an active part in, non-Catholic worship (canon 1258). With the Second Vatican Council, a new ecumenical and inter-faith awareness gradually became established, but problems with dialogue and with religious freedom still remained dominant notes in the Roman Catholic tradition, obstructing a greater receptivity to the new signs of the times. The same approach was evident in reaction to the event in Assisi. Certain writers analysed the ambiguities present in the event as an expression of the problems and contradictions that have always marked the relations between Christianity and other religions, including during the pontificate of John Paul II.[19]

The greatest fear provoked by the preparation for and execution of the day in Assisi concerned the danger of syncretism. To prevent any suspicion of syncretism, any initiative that might have allowed for inter-faith prayer was avoided. The most determined opposition, as Marcelo Zago has pointed out, stressed precisely this risk of syncretism, of a mixture between Christianity and other religions and a risk of confusing truth and error. Hence the extreme care taken by the planners at all stages of the event, particularly at the third stage of the day, to avoid any feature or format that could have given rise to an erroneous interpretation.[20]

Despite all the precautions taken, adverse reactions still followed. For the conservative Bishop Marcel Lefebvre, who since 1983 had been denouncing Pope John Paul II's more open initiatives in the spheres of ecumenism and inter-faith dialogue, the gathering in Assisi constituted a 'public blasphemy' and a scandal, a living expression of the heretical degeneration of conciliar Roman Catholicism.[21] Other more subtle criticism came from officials in parts of the Roman Curia, equally dissatisfied with the significance and the repercussions of the event. Following the usual lines of his missiological vision, forcefully expressed in his book *Rapporto sulla fede* (1985), Cardinal Joseph Ratzinger showed no greater enthusiasm for the experience, preferring to maintain a 'more than lukewarm reservation'.[22] Other critical voices came from more specifically theological directions, such as that of Henry van Straelen, who saw the event as being marginal to the church.[23]

The objections expressed during and after the event provoked two explicit interventions from the pope, one addressed to the Roman Curia, in

December 1986, and the other to the Diplomatic Corps accredited to the Holy See, in January 1987. In the first address, the pope reminded his colleagues that the day in Assisi had been the most widely reported religious event of the whole of 1986. He pointed out that the sole content of the day had been prayer, seen as an essential constituent in the achievement of peace. He stressed the unique character of the event, a 'visible illustration' of the whole 'ecumenical thrust for inter-faith dialogue recommended and provided for by Vatican II'.[24] For the more alert analysts, it was clear that these speeches by the pope were intended to justify and 'defend a principle and an experience', but the climate of ecclesiastical thinking dominant at the time did not favour a more appreciative reception of the event or a guarantee that it would have any influence over time.[25]

III. A paradigm and a sign of the times

The Assisi day of prayer is paradigmatic in that it effectively produced a deep break with the traditional posture of the Catholic Church on inter-faith dialogue. Despite the strategic conditions imposed so as to avoid difficulties, the experience itself produced a unique novelty. And it is this novelty that provoked and still provokes resistance on the part of all integralists, for whom the mystery of God is enclosed within a single religious experience. In harmony with a general tendency in theology today, the event in Assisi pointed to a new sensitivity as well as to a new understanding of the radical nature of Christianity as it faces the challenge of religious pluralism. Religious diversity has ceased to be seen as a threat to Christian faith and is seen rather as the living expression of the multiform riches of the mystery of God.

In continuity with the spirit and ecumenical and inter-faith dynamic of Vatican II, the gathering in Assisi provided a landmark in proclaiming a new attitude of respect toward other religious traditions. This approach has been much evidenced in John Paul II's speeches: respect for the diversified search for the mystery of God, recognition of the value of obeying one's conscience and of authentic prayer. He has also expressed a deep understanding of a unity underlying diversity, a unity that is radical and determining but does not extinguish understanding of the presence of spiritual riches granted by God to different peoples. The outstanding impression made by the Assisi gathering was a deep unity inspiring all those who look to religion and spiritual values for an answer to the great challenges and questions facing human hearts, as well as a common aspiration to peace as a universal requirement. The times and the forms of inter-faith dialogue are punctuated by

'God's patience' and by the silent and imponderable action of the Spirit, who continues to open hearts and minds so that antagonisms may be overcome in the interests of mutual enrichment. The gathering at Assisi was a small but significant sign of greater communion, 'an anticipation of what God would want the course of human histiry to be: a companionable journey on which we accompany one another on the way to the transcendent goal he has set for us'.[26]

The recent publication of the Declaration *Dominus Iesus* has dealt a blow to this spirit of Assisi. In relation to earlier documents issued by the Congregation for the Doctrine of the Faith, it says nothing really new. It fits well into the dynamic of 'restoration', inspired by the same concern for identity found in previous letters or declarations from this Roman dicastery. The impact made by *Dominus Iesus* in secular and religious circles is due to the harsh tone expressed in its language. But it also reflects a many-sided fear: of relativism, of indifferentism, of reduction of content of faith, of a new reform of the church . . . and also fear of the theological consequences and implications of a closer approach to other faith communities – in particular, dread of discovering that God may speak in various ways, being gift of grace and permanent surprise. There is a clear collision here between the Declaration and the spirit that inspired it and the dialogal gestures made by John Paul II.[27]

The difficulties, resistance, and barriers raised make the progress of interfaith dialogue more problematical, but they cannot prevent its affirmation in history. This is one of the most important and essential features of our age. Dialogue does not suffocate religious convictions but reveals new and unexpected dimensions of the mystery of God. As John Paul II stated, after the publication of *Dominus Iesus*, the spirit of Assisi cannot be extinguished but has to 'spread throughout the world, everywhere encouraging new witnesses to peace and dialogue'. At this time of hardening of ethnic and religious conflicts the world has most need of peace and dialogue, of a more authentic relationship with the Absolute, one that brings more life and humanity to all. The spirit of Assisi is 'a providential gift to our times' and must act as an inspiration for greater daring along the route of dialogue, so that 'the men and women of this world, whatever race or creed they belong to, can discover themselves to be children of God and brothers and sisters of one another'.[28]

Translated by Paul Burns

Notes

1. Dalai Lama, *An Ethic for the New Millennium*, London 2000; id., *Goodness of Heart*, London 1997.

2. John Paul II, encyclical *Ut Unum Sint*, 1995, n. 76.

3. F. Boespflug, 'Assise, une signe prophétique?', in F. Boespflug and Y. Labbé (eds), *Assise, dix ans après, 1986–1996*, Paris 1996, p.67; A. Melloni, 'La rencontre d'Assise et ses développements dans la dynamique du Concile Vatican II', in J. Doré (ed), *Le Christianisme vis-à-vis des religions*, Namur 1997, p.99; M. Amaladoss, *Rinnovare tutte le cose*, Rome 1993, p.124.

4. M.-D. Chenu, 'Pour une écumenisme planetaire', *L'actualité religieuse dans le monde* 38 (1986), pp.21–3.

5. Pontifical Council for Inter-Faith Dialogue, *Diálogo e Anúncio*, Petrópolis 1991, n. 5. A. Melloni has pointed to the similarity between the Assisi gesture and some important works in the field of theology of religions, by H. Küng, J. Dupuis and D. Tracy: see 'La rencontre' (n.3), p.116.

6. M. Zago, 'Day of Prayer for Peace', Secretarius pro Non Christianis, *Bulletin* 22 (1987), p.150; M. Amaladoss, *Pela estrada da vida*, São Paulo 1996, p.10.

7. John Paul II, 'Le dialogue interreligieux est devenu réalité – message au cardinal Edward Idriss Cassidy pour la XIIIme Rencontre "Hommes et religions" à Lisbonne', *La Documentation Catholique* 2236 (2000), pp.957–8.

8. *La Documentation Catholique* 1913 (1986), pp. 233–5.

9. A. Pintarelli, *O espírito de Assis*, Petrópolis 1996, pp.22–3.

10. C. Geffré, *Passion de l'homme, passion de Dieu*, Paris 1991, p.124. For Geffré, the day at Assisi was, for those who know how to read the signs of the times, a 'historic day in the religious history of humankind'. It was a 'considerable spiritual event', the great lesson of which concerns the 'ecumenical outreach of prayer': see 'La prière des hommes comme mystère de gratuité', *La Vie Spirituelle* 726 (1998), p.125.

11. The concern to avoid any risk of syncretism was present in the pope's words during a general audience before the event: 'On the esplanade of the lower basilica of St Francis, the prayers of the representatives of each religion will be made separately, one after the other, while all the others will *assist*, through an inward and outward show of respect, in the witness of men and women in their supreme effort to seek God': John Paul II, 'Ai fedeli in audienza generale', Pontifical Council for Inter-Faith Dialogue, *Il dialogo interreligioso nel magisterio pontificio*, Vatican City 1994, p.404. The choice of the verb 'assist' (my italics) is most significant.

12. E. Balducci, *L'uomo planetario*, Fiesole 1994, p.164.

13. M. Amaladoss, 'Prier ensemble pour la paix. Assise dans le contexte d'aujourd'hui', *Spiritus* 126 (1992), pp.111–2.

14. John Paul II, 'Alla curia romana', in *Il dialogo* (n.11), pp.429–30. And a little further on he reiterates, 'Differences constitute a less important element than unity, which, on the contrary, is radical, basic, and determining', p.431.

15. Ibid., p.437.

16. Secretariat for Non-Believers, 'O cristianismo e as outras religiões', *Sedoc* 17 (1984), pp.395–6.

17. Amaladoss, *Pela estrada*, pp.87–8. Reflecting on the subject of what unites Christianity and Islam, Claude Geffré stressed that it was not wrong to affirm the existence of a community of faith in the transcendence of a single personal God. It is the same God who is adored, but 'with a different understanding of his oneness': C. Geffré, 'La portée thélogique du dialogue islamo-chrétien', *Islamochristiana* 18 (1992), p.16; see also J. Dupuis, *Rumo a una teologia cristã do pluralismo religioso*, São Paulo 1999, p.523.

18. John Paul II, 'Ai rappresentanti delle varie religioni', in *Il dialogo* (n.11), p.413.

19. Melloni, 'La rencontre' (n.3), pp.195, 114.

20. F. Wernert, 'Assise, un rassemblement liturgique?', in *Assise, dix ans après*, 97, n. 2.

21. L. Perrin, *L'affaire Lefebvre*, Paris 1990, pp.34, 76.

22. Melloni, 'La rencontre' (n.3), p.117.

23. H. van Straelen, *L'Eglise et les religions non chrétiennes au seuil du XXI siècle*, Paris 1994, pp.305–6. Echoing difficulties expressed in various quarters, he asks how widely the Assisi gathering might have given the impression that all religions were equal, or played down the importance of missionary work. At one point he asks what sense there is in the presence of non-Christians and their rites in Catholic buildings. In the end, he accepts that the experience might have given religious leaders 'the desire to know the true God' (sic!).

24. John Paul II, 'Alla curia romana', in *Il dialogo* (n.11), p.434. In this same address, the pope had stressed that the appropriate reading key for understanding the event was to be found in the teaching of Vatican II: ibid., p.430.

25. In Melloni's view, the resistance to and criticism of the Assisi event would block 'a segment of papal action for the foreseeable future' (n.3), p.118.

26. John Paul II, 'Ai rappresentanti delle varie religioni', p.416.

27. In October 1999, on the occasion of the closure of the Inter-Faith Assembly held in Rome, the pope had stressed that interest in dialogue among the religions formed one of the 'signs of hope present in the last part of this century', a hope that 'the gift of the Holy Spirit, who calls us to broaden our horizons': John Paul II, speech during meeting with leaders of various religions, *Oss. Rom.* 47 (1999), p.10. For a reflection on the Declaration *Dominus Iesus* see F. Teixeira, 'Do diálogo al anúncio', *REB* 240 (2000).

28. John Paul II, 'Le dialogue interreligieux est devenu réalité' (n.7), p.958.

Ecumenical Gestures in Contemporary Catholicism

ALBERTO MELLONI

The copious documentation on the ecumenical movement of the twentieth century has shown how the heart of this experience, spread across several generations of Christians, has been the effort to explore the real extent of the fundamental disagreement that characterized the separated churches. The differences between them – held to be incompatible with truths of faith, sanctioned in solemn acts, consolidated by theological systems, marked by condemnations – could not be explained and so built up into a system of mutual mistrust. The ecumenical movement set out to explore precisely these separations, using the tools of honest and respectful theological confrontation, to evaluate their nature without adversarial aggressiveness, to consider the space for complementarity among legitimate differences in the expressions of faith, and to seek a visibile unity in communion.[1]

The position adopted by the Roman Catholic Church toward this current evolved to a marked degree during the course of the twentieth century,[2] until it took the shape of an irrevocable ecumenical endeavour, inscribed by John XXIII in the heart of curial government when he instituted the Secretariat for Christian Unity, and which the Second Vatican Council formally raised to the universal level with the decree on ecumenism, *Unitatis redintegratio*.[3] This endeavour has been repeatedly confirmed by pontifical authority throughout the post-conciliar period and has become a paradigm (or a parable) of the reception of the council. Basic stages in this process – *Tomos Agapis*, BEM, ARCIC I, the Augsburg agreement – have marked moments of real progress in the direction of unity[4] and have often also provoked adverse reactions. Frequently (and not only on the Roman side), people have acted and argued as though the whole ecumenical endeavour were contained in dialogue – and theological dialogue at that – so that they have acted and reacted as though their progress or lack of it could be governed by levers pulled by theologians, by their words, their writings, their teachings and commentaries.

In actuality another factor has been to the fore throughout many years of ecumenism: that of *gestures*, in which the Roman Catholic Church has played its part. The level of gesture has been important over a long period and still is in the current historical and political climate. The use of gestures, of course, is far from absent in Christian tradition, which notably recognizes and ritualizes movements, postures, clothing, both in its acts of worship and in its processes of government. To show commitment to unity by means of gestures is therefore one way of sending messages and signals that make a geat impact at all levels in the church. All the more so, from the post-war period on, because information media have made it possible to transmit not only texts and voices but images and figures with ever-increasing speed: on the level of *political* communication in the broad sense, gesture has become a sort of counterweight either supporting or contradicting or even bringing about the words of acts of government. The peculiarity of the ecclesiological structure of Catholicism and the over-exposure of the pope to the media, which has grown over the whole of the twentieth century, have therefore lent a particular importance to some of its ecumenical gestures, judged by some to mark a 'change' that cannot fail to have repercussions on conceptions of what it means to be a church, by others to represent the metamorphosis of a power capable of modernizing itself while still clinging on to its power.

Division in gestures

To understand ecumenical gestures we need first to recall what they are differentiated from and then what their purpose is. The first thing to say is that ecumenical gestures reverse the corresponding repertoire of gestures of opposition that have punctuated the history of division among Christians.

Gestures as such are hardly a twentieth-century invention and are well attested (in their capacity to actualize and reveal collective states of mind) throughout the different phases of division: conciliar as well as papal ceremonial has often associated decisions to condemn and excommunicate with emblematic gestures (some of which have become legendary). Bulls laid on altars, extinguishing of candles, torchlight processions by the people have been part of the choreography of so many instances of inability to hold on to communion and truth. And even in relatively recent years Pius IX beating his feet against 'this hard head' of Patriarch Yussef, found guilty of not agreeing *passivamente* with the majority in favour of infallibility at Vatican I,[5] has been a sign of a desire for sovereign power on the part of the pope of Rome, which was totally unacceptabe to non-Catholics and virtuously taken for granted by Catholics.

What was new for the Roman Catholic Church in the twentieth century was that in the upper reaches of the hierarchy certain gestures became solemn and irreversible occasions for declaring a *de facto* communion still distant *in dialogo*. No analytical examination of these gestures, of their parallels and the expectation to which they have given rise in other confessional circles in the history of the ecumenical movement has been made; nor has any assessment of ecumenical gestures at grassroots level been undertaken.[6] It is therefore not possible to attempt a comprehensive pre-history here, but only to evoke occasions when and places where experience of the communion possible among Christians has been glimpsed and to state that critical assessments of these are still inadequate. It is, for example, often said that the experience of wars allowed divided Christians to come together in the suffering and deprivation of the camps shared by soldiers divided by confessions of faith but united in a common plight; while, however, this is something familiar on the level of general statement, documented by so many memories of prisoners of war and by episodes put into thousands of biographies, it has still not been described (and perhaps never can be) as a whole. The same has been said of sufferings shared in the gulags and in the prisons of the People's Republics in the period following the Second World War by Christians of different and unreconciled denominations. Other examples could be given – such as the role played by the fragile autocephalous Orthodox churches of the Balkans in blunting the arrogance of Latin demands for union or smoothing the particular situation of the post-Ottoman world.

Gestures of encounter

The receding pre-history of desire for unity, which also affects Roman Catholicism, reached an end point in the pontificate of John XXIII, who made gestures an instrument of a public and visible – and therefore irreversible – undertaking. It was he who exploited what was one of the most cumbersome principles of an intransigent conception of the papacy – that of institutional continuity, which within certain limits prevents a pope from modifying the positions adopted by a predecessor – by making 'definitive' gestures of communion, points of no return in the quest for communion and brotherhood.

The gestures made by John XXIII were gestures of *encounter*. Roncalli saw encounter not as the preface or prelude to a dialogue that then had to be undertaken on the theological level, but as the rediscovery of a condition, that of confessing that the gift of God unites 'fatherhood and brotherhood', as he was to say in the evening of 11 October 1962.[7]

His was a choice that did not derive from any sort of direct and continual militancy within the ecumenical movement:[8] it was only in 1925, when Roncalli was despatched as apostolic visitor to Bulgaria, that experience of Christian divisions became part of his direct experience and of his reading. In Sofia and then during the ten years he spent in Istanbul as apostolic delegate from 1935 to 1944, a step from the Phanar and from the Armenian patriarchate, Roncalli pondered the need for an ecumenism that would not be just that of theological dialogue: in Bulgaria he visited the Orthodox synod on several occasions, and on the Bosphorus he was to involve the metropolitans of sister churches and the Chief Rabbi in two joint celebrations, for the funeral of Pius XI and the election of Pius XII in 1939.[9] On the other hand it cannot be said that Roncalli derived his concept of gestures from any sort of commitment to 'spiritual ecumenism' (as preached by Fr Dumont), which, as Étienne Fouilloux has shown, has been the least fruitful on the complex journey undertaken in the twentieth century: Roncalli's ecumenism was not one of worthy sentiments with any fulfilment lazily put off 'until God wills'.[10]

The effect of any fragment of ecumenical theology that recognizes that what binds those who believe in Christ together, the impact of any spiritual optimism rooted in the conviction that what unites is qualitatively more significant that what divides, creates space for gestures of encounter. Such was Roncalli's verbal promise when he left Bulgaria in 1934, when he declared that any Bulgarian brother passing by his house at any time would not be asked whether he was Catholic or Orthodox but would be met 'with a brotherly embrace and the heart of a friend'.[11] This promise was to be made visible and receive public confirmation when Roncalli was elected pope on 28 October 1958.

The brotherhood he envisaged was to be given space in the style of his papacy, and so space was made for gestures: gestures toward the poor (Rome's prisoners and sick), gestures toward non-Catholics; the consensus such ecumenical gestures provoked in public opinion smoothed the way to the creation of the Secretariat for Christian Unity, suggested and then directed by Cardinal Augustine Bea.[12] I recall the most significant stages in this didactic process.

The first was a simple gesture, the audience granted to the Orthodox Metropolitan Jakovos (Koukuozis) in March 1959. The pope received this 'representative' of the throne of Andrew at a critical moment for synodal dialectic within the Phanar,[13] but he did not want to lose the chance of a occasion for making contact. The dialogue between them was no bombshell (Jakovos was to relate that in his conversation with the pope the latter recognized that blame for the separation between East and West should be shared *equally* by both sides of divided Christendom), but the signal had been given, and it reached the churches.

Then the audience with the Archbishop of Canterbury, Geoffrey Fisher, in December 1960, had no very special content. The meeting between Pope John and the man the *Osservatore Romano* pointedly referred to as 'Doctor' Fisher (it had been 563 years since the titulars of the two sees had spoken to one another . . .) had come about thanks to the promptness with which Fisher had accepted an indirect suggestion from Roncalli: the pope had advisd him, through the embassy of a common interlocutor, to pay a visit to the patriarchs of Sofia, Bucharest, Constantinople, and Athens and to come on to Rome. Fisher accepted the advice, and his visit changed a whole climate.[14] There was no agenda, and so no possibility of success or failure: for Fisher it was important that the pope (who in private conversation had unwittingly spoken of the *return* of the other churches) should have allowed himself to be corrected by his Anglican colleague and to recognize that *unity* was the duty and command laid on all; for Roncalli, what counted was for them to have been seen and noticed.[15]

These small gestures of encounter helped to make up the great gesture of the council, announced on 25 January 1959 with a decidedly ecumenical outlook: from that first moment John XXIII did not want to invite the other Christians to a round-table examination of doctrinal differences, nor lead them into a snare in which papal paternalism would be exalted and the other churches forced to keep their distance by withdrawing from a dangerous embrace. The invitation was to take part together in the 'banquet of grace', almost in a joint quest for a common confession of the possibility of unity.[16] The audiences lent substance to the invitation: they prepared and anticipated the realization of that encounter, which thanks to the birth of the Secretariat for Christian Unity was to become truly real, despite the incidents that punctuated the preparations for its work from 1959 to 1962.

Extraneous and perhaps even fortuitous elements are known to have accounted for the wide presence of observers from other churches (including that of Moscow) at the opening of Vatican II: but for Roncalli this was the proof that encounter has a power of its own.[17] The council – as being more than individual gestures – was for Pope John an experience that was meaningful for its very existence, in ecumenical terms as well. Encounter is encounter, communion is communion, to the degree that can be experienced in a particular theological climate and at a specific disciplinary stage: the gesture is the wager of a possibility of communion as a foretaste of brotherhood and trust essential to, not merely leading to, theological dialogue – as was to be seen when Pope John died (3 June 1963), an event surrounded by the ecumenical miracle of consensus without triumphalism.

Liturgical gestures

With Paul VI, elected to carry John's council forward, ecumenical gestures acquired an autonomy of their own in relation to the council: they grew in both scope and significance. While Roncalli had been the serene architect of *encounter* as a theologically important action, Montini, in his turn, was the passionate engineer of gesture as an instrument of ecumenical *dialogue*.[18] For him, gesture could not be complete in welcoming the other as such but involved recognizing the other as Christian. Dialogue (which, to a certain extent, discounts irreducibility of difference) is born in ecumenical gestures, into which Montini introduced a further element (typical of papal audiences), that of gifts. And these gifts became central and powerful focus of the gestures because they pointed to a theological horizon.

The first occasion on which this step forward was taken was during the meeting between the pope and the patriarch of Constantinople, which took place in Jerusalem at the beginning of January 1964. Paul VI's decision to undertake the first papal pilgrimage to the Holy Land – in the midst of unresolved theological and political problems – took on a great charge of ecumenical content, not when it was being planned but when Athenagoras decided to travel to the Holy City in order to receive and talk to the pope of Rome. The reservations, especially on the Greek side, were well known to both participants, and they constituted a threat, which Athenagoras elegantly circumvented. When journalists asked him if 'the theologians were in agreement' about the meeting, the patriarch replied, 'I don't know, because there are so many theologians; what I do know is what theology states: that there is only one theology.'[19]

Conscious of the close attention being paid to it, those who devised the protocol of the meeting were careful not to give any impression of giving way or weakness on the part of either party.[20] Nevertheless, once they were face to face with one another, Paul VI and Athenagoras abandoned caution and moved directly to those liturgical gestures that the New Testament describes as necessary for communion. The pope and the patriarch, under the gaze, this time, of TV cameras and of reporters, exchanged the embrace of peace and the sacred kiss. What happened on 5 January 1964 was not just an episode but the first proof that gesture produces and expresses more than words privately spoken between two people, however friendly, can convey.[21]

The next day, almost as if to confirm that the reciprocal acceptance of codiscipleship, *mathiaktoume*, as Athenagoras defined it, had *already* produced a degree of unity, an even more significant exchange of gifts took place. The patriarch placed the *engolpion*, the medallion that is the sign of Orthodox episcopal dignity, round Pope Paul's neck: the Orthodox faithful present (who were by no means hand-picked) showed thir approval by acclaiming the pope of Rome as *axiòs*, as in episcopal consecrations. For his part, Paul VI offered Athenagoras a chalice for eucharistic celebration (later handed back to him by the patriarch, who some days later had wine sent from Patmos with which to celebrate the eucharist).[22] This was followed by an alternate reading of the seventeenth chapter of John's Gospel in Greek, which crowned this unity in act as all that it could be. Just as the patriarch of Constantinople was convinced that the ecumenical *kairòs* of Catholicism assembled in council would not be spoilt for any reason on earth, so the pope of Rome felt the need to show that his desire to share the common chalice marked a point from which there was no drawing back. Paul VI brought out not the peripheral differences between the two confessions but the central one: they had not reached the *fait accompli* of intercommunion, but the reciprocal acceptance of the chalice had been shown to be a *necessary* horizon to the truth of dialogue itself.

No less significant was the exchange of gifts between Paul VI and Archbishop Michael Ramsey of Canterbury, who came to pay him a visit in Rome. Ramsey met Paul VI in a series of audiences and sessions of joint prayer on 23 and 24 March 1966. Expectations were much higher than at the pre-conciliar audience with John XXIII, and the questions at issue were far more direct, though on this level the results were unquestionably modest. The questions dealt with – including the invalidity of Anglican ordination decreed by Leo XIII – were not such as could be disposed of simply through goodwill: on the Catholic side, Paul VI frankly admitted that the problem was how to move forward in communion without contradicting a pontifical decision that had become obsolete in practice but was still felt to be unchangeable.[23] And on this point the right words still have to be found.

At the end of the audience, the exchange of gifts went well beyond what verbal communication had been able to achieve – and perhaps even beyond what the ecumenical officials had planned. Ramsey presented the pope with his pectoral cross, the sign of the giver's episcopal rank, as the pope recognized as such in the act of putting it on, and he then, perhaps unexpectedly, replied by offering Ramsey his episcopal ring, the *anulus piscatorius*, around which the Middle Ages had built a complex symbolical system.[24] The archbishop placed this sign of apostolic jurisdiction on his finger with understandable hope, as though it were an unexpected and meaningful surpise.[25]

With respect to the heavy obstacle represented by Leo XIII's wording, these liturgical gifts sought to shed that 'new light' Montini glimpsed, in a search for a way of overcoming the blockage formed by now obsolete ecumenical illiteracy and still paralysing magisterial concepts. The gesture and its reciprocation formed one way of moving forward.

A third particularly significant ecumenical gesture made by Paul VI was the one he made on the tenth aniversary of the exchange of the *Tomos agapis*. This solemn act, signed on 7 December 1965 between the Phanar and Rome, reciprocally repealing the excommunications between the throne of Andrew and that of Peter, had not been framed as a simple gesture: there were those who proposed an ecumenical 'grand finale' to Vatican II (Mgr Camara even put forward an appropiate scenario for acts of pardon and reconciliation among Catholics, among Christians, among believers, among all people). Likewise, the suggestion made by Metropolitan Meliton of Hilioupolis, for a solemn and formal act cancelling the excommunications of 1054 – a gesture that had to lead to a eucharistic table shared by pope and patriarch, by metropolitans and bishops – was, thanks to the work of theologians, shown to be impracticable and reduced to a common declaration. Athenagoras could not put Orthodox unity at risk: if he jumped steps toward communion, the reservations of Maximos of Sardis, who lamented the lack of coordination with other Orthodox churches in ecumenical matters, would have become explosive. Paul VI, for his part, was still determined to assimilate the objections of the unruly minority at Vatican II, and no one encouraged him make a break, even *in extremis*, with the style of government he had assumed at the beginning of his papacy. This was why the *Tomos agapis* became also and above all a text and act, but not a gesture in the strong sense: it also became a text (underlined after the end of the council by a solemn liturgy celebrated on the feast of St Ambrose, common to both calendars) that abrogates the reciprocal condemnations like a ladder reaching up to the skies. A text without a gesture, the *Tomos* placed Orthodoxy and Catholicism in a unique situation of non-excommunication and non-communion. Doctrinal condemnations had for centuries been the ditch dug by the division but also the basis of the division itself: with these removed, it was up to the churches to decide whether and how to proceed to the actual reforms necessary if they were to move from non-excommunication to full communion. A long and difficult process of research was put in train, with other meetings and dialogues, and Paul VI decided to take a personal initiative designed to move things forward.

In the course of the ceremony in the Sistine Chapel, Paul VI bent to kiss the foot of Metropolitan Meliton, who was co-presiding the service in the name of the ecumenical patriarch:[26] it was a sign of penitence, of asking forgiveness, and also an overturning of the sign of sovereignty imposed by the papal court (from the eighth century down to and including the reign of Pius XII) on those who arrived in the pope's presence. This gesture of humiliation before a sovereign power thus became a sort of sign of penitence on the part of the papacy and of a hope for communion.

Gestures without theology?

The judgment on these gestures in historical and theological writings has been either hurried or emotional: the mass of results of dialogue has more or less reduced them to a pleonastic adjunct to the decisive level, seen as what has been noted in theological analysis of the questions and the search for agreements.[27] There has been a sort of blurring of the memory of a question that, at the time it was raised, disturbed such a leading theologian of the ecumenical movement as Yves M.-J. Congar, a supremely qualified observer and one beyond all suspicion of sentimentality.[28] His initial judgment was marked with diffidence. This diffidence applied to all the gestures made by John XXIII: for Congar, the overall tone of Roncalli's could be seen in this way. Faced with the general reaction to John XXIII's death, the Dominican theologian observed:

> All at once the immense echo produced by this humble, good man was shown. It was seen that he had profoundly altered the religious and even human map of the world: simply by being what he was. He did not work through great systems of ideas, but through gestures and a certain personal style. He did not speak in the name of the system, of its legitimacy, of its authority, but simply in the name of intuitions and of the impulse of a heart that on the one hand obeyed God and on the other loved people, or rather did both from the same impulse.[29]

Pope John's gestures would then, according to Congar, have been an alternative to setting out ideas: so his whole pontificate would have been innovative just on the basis of this unique double movement of clinging to God and to people, *fait* as well as *accompli*.

Congar's doubts were perhaps fairly strong when it came to evaluating the gestures made by Paul VI. From his diary of the council one can see that on 4 June 1964 Congar contrasted the *presence* of ecumenical gestures in the pope's actions (even the smallest ones that cannot be reconstructed here[30]) with the *lack* of a theology of these very gestures, which struck him as indispensable. This was a judgment that was to be repeated and refined over many months. It first appeared during a discourse with Mgr Poupard in the Secretariat of State: a few months after the historic embrace between Athenagoras and Paul VI in Jerusalem, the Dominican insisted 'on saying that the pope's gestures, which created a new situation from the ecumenical point of view, lacked the ecclesiological basis required of them. What was needed was an ecclesiology of the church as a communion of churches. Neither has the liturgical movement the ecclesiological basis it needs. We make movements of overture, but we are working with a markedly medieval and Counter-Reformation ecclesiology, which is totally inadequate.'[31]

This was not one of those malicious undercurrents common in the Roman environment but a thesis that Congar wanted to present directly to Paul VI himself, so as to put him on his guard against making the *fait accompli* too easy. But before he had a chance to do so, he burned his own diagnostic notes: in November 1964 the pope intervened heavily in the council's workings, commanding that some modifications be made by the concilar majority in order to placate an insubordinate minority.[32] Congar saw such a procedure as deriving from an ecclesiological *lacuna* that clashed with the ecumenical overtures: on 15 November he wrote: 'I see once more that the pope does not have the ecclesiology to support his grand ecumenical gestures.' His discussion with one the best-informed Belgian theologians, Albert Prignon, rector of the Belgian college in Rome, confirmed the thesis Congar had worked out: 'Prignon agrees that the pope absolutely lacks the ecclesiology of his gestures. He once asked himself just how far can we go in making "concessions" to the Orthodox. Under such conditions, dialogue is, humanly speaking, still-born!' (17 Nov.). When on 19 November it was learned that papal hesitations had modified the documents under discussion at the council, including the final wording of the decree on ecumenism, Congar asked himself:

> Ecumenism is at stake. [. . .] But I react very quickly: so? What of the embrace in Jerusalem? Was that play-acting? Would the pope make gestures and nothing more? He can't have the theology of his gestures at all: in fact he must have a contrary theology. We shall see. I don't want to get caught up in what might be imagination. I also tell myself I am not praying enough; I am not carrying the struggle forward on the spiritual level. [. . .] There is no doubt that this morning has been *catastrophic* from the point of view of the ecumenical climate. It is clear that the pope makes

grand symbolical gestures but that behind these there is neither the theology nor the practical understanding of what these gestures would bring about.[33]

Congar was not prepared to smooth over or forget about the problems that worried him. But neither was he insensitive to the answers that might be found. And one persuasive answer, which he accepted in all seriousness, was provided by Fr Pierre Duprey on 14 September 1965. Faced with the news brought to him from Russia by this most active official of the Secretariat for Christian Unity on the success achieved by the pope's messages, Congar repeated that 'the problem, for me, is that the pope should have the theology of his gestures and his messages'. Duprey, however, suggested a reading that he judged 'interesting and true':

> We must, he said, let the pope and Rome make gestures and address messages, even if the thinking is not yet up to their level. Because it will follow one day. If we were now to *formulate* the implications of these gestures and messages, it is probable that Rome would recoil in the face of such a formulation of ideas. The gestures will provide a period of acclimatization at the end of which, one day, the formulas will be acceptable. And this does not apply to Rome only. With the Orthodox, too, the theologians have not caught up with the present ecumenical situation. They too would benefit from a period of familiarization, starting from things as they actually are.[34]

Congar, trusting in Duprey's words, then accepted the idea of attention to the provisional nature of gestures, as propaedeutic and therapeutic acts: in the silence of their making, they form an 'implicit' basis, which can later, at the stage of research into the 'formulas' needed, be rendered 'explicit'.[35] The inadequacy of the thinking to be found above all at the highest level of the hierarchy does not mean that ecumenical gestures are out of place but, on the contrary, makes them necessary, given the urgency of the situation and the opportunities history has provided for uniting the churches. This view has had no visible effects, but it seems to me to mark the emergence of an understanding and of a legitimation on which many gestures have depended over the years.

Postconciliar experience

Between the end of the council and the present the ecumenical scene has certainly changed considerably, including the impression made by 'the pope and Rome', seen in 1965 as still unprovided with thinking adequate to deal with the ecumenical challenges facing them. With John Paul II, ecumenical gestures too have changed in significance and intent from the days of John XXIII and Paul VI. As in many other aspects, the pontificate of Karol Wojtyla has changed the style of papal government, not just in its apparently increased exercise.[36] The outpouring of words and the use made of televisual technique have produced contradictions that worry theologians. For the people, however, who have become an audience, papal gestures count more than words: one only has to think – in inter-religious relations – of what the Assisi pilgrimage in 1986 meant, or the presence of the pope dressed as a Christian penitent at the Western Wall in Jerusalem in 2000. At the same time, gestures infinitely multiplied – and this applies particularly to ecumenical ones, which have become a standard component of all papal journeys and which finally became part of the opening liturgy for Jubilee 2000 in the basilica of St Paul without the Walls – risk affirming the irrevocability of an undertaking without hastening the steps along the road, for which the pontiff appeals for help and counsel (solemnly in the encyclical *Ut unum sint*, with sorrowful words on various journeys).

The proliferation of encounters, the exchanges of gifts, the gestures of brotherhood and respect the pope unfailingly makes with respect are producing a possible and limited communion. The nature and the repetition of such gestures, however, serve to sharpen the question Congar asked himself in the time of Paul VI: what is the theology of such gestures? Are we simply attending a baroque replay of the rhetoric of a unity that does not exist? Are the gestures witness of the slow maturing or of the spectacular polluting of the desire for unity that the gospel kindles in the hearts of believers?

In order to answer that question without rhetorical short cuts or facile sarcasm, one has immediately to make clear that the context of ecumenical dialogue is different today, as is the place gestures occupy in relation to dialogue. Meetings of ecumenists from the various churches – bilateral and multilateral, inside and outside *CEC* – have produced great successes.[37] Significant, even if sporadic, episodes (such as the pope's recital of the Creed in Greek without the *filioque* on the fourteen-hundredth anniversary of the Council of Constantinople) have shown that, not least on the Roman side, the thick doctrinal walls of division can be breached. And even the most unfortunate failures – such as the failure of ARCIC I or the letter from the Congregation for the Doctrine of the Faith to the presidents of episcopal conferences forbidding them to borrow the expression 'sister churches' from the papal magisterium – have been products of circumstances and of perceptions of the historical *kairos* so modest as not even to have understood, let alone deepened, the arguments put forward in dialogue. Not even the wounding opposition among the churches over the ministerial role of believers of the feminine gender – in which reasons for distance and conflict have been constructed *ex novo* – has been able to interrupt the theological discussion. And yet this undoubted success itself points to the intrinsic limitation of dialogue as an instrument: that 'any document that establishes a consensus on the theological condition is acceptable, but on condition that it does not, by its nature, require a decisive step forward that affects the way the churches are structured here and now'. To call this a blind alley is a not unduly crude way of putting it: it neither can nor would wish to under-estimate the importance of the road travelled to reach it.[38]

This actual state of dialogue, then, gives a different significance to gestures and assigns them a different place from that proposed by Duprey and Congar in that dawn of Catholic ecumenism in 1965. The fact is that if at that time gestures *rather than* dialogue established implicit and un-explored levels of communion, today fraternal gestures made by heads of churches also reveal *the same* weakness of dialogue:[39]we can make all these gestures of mutual respect and brotherhood, exchange the most meaningful and precious gifts, share experiences of great depth – everything except celebrate communion at a shared table.[40]

So have the gestures of the council years been swallowed up by inflation in the course of the reception of Vatican II?

Translated by Paul Burns

Notes

1. Cf. H. E. Fey, *The Ecumenical Advance. The History of the Ecumenical Movement*, 2, London 1970, and an updating in E. Fouilloux, 'Histoires d'Ecuménisme', in *Revue d'histoire ecclésiastique* 95, 3 (2000), pp.489–503.

2. E. Fouilloux, *Les catholiques et l'unité chrétienne du XIXme au XXme siècle. Itinéraires françaises*, Paris 1982.

3. M. Velati, *Una difficile transizione. Il cattolecismo e l'unità cristiana dagli Cinquanta al Vaticano II*, Bologna, 1996, in *Storia del concilio Vaticano II*, dir. G. Alberigo, ed A. Melloni, 5 vols., Bologna 1995–2001.

4. Cf. S. Voicu, G. Cereti, J. Puglisi (eds), *Enchiridion oecumenicum*, Bologna 1986ff.

5. See the account in G. M. Croce (ed), *Una fonte importante per la storia del pontificato di Pio IX e del Concilio Vaticano I: i manoscritti inediti di Vincenzo Tizzani*, extract in vols of *Archivum Historiae Pontificiae e Roma*, 1985–7.

6. Those aspects on which I dwell here are of course not the only ecumenical

gestures: missionary and charitable co-operation and common sufferings in war and captivity have created situations in which many acts of communion have been accomplished by the faithful out of faithfulness to the gospel and not merely from impatience with confessional antagonism; on the Catholic side, the years following Vatican II have, *a fortiori*, strengthened this experience, leading to the practice of intercommunion in some monastic and lay circles; the whole of this sphere, however, is fraught with bibliographical and, even more, heuristic problems.

7. *Storia del concilio Vaticano II*, 2, pp.38–41.

8. G. Alberigo, *Papa Giovanni*, Bologna 2000, with relevant bibliography.

9. Cf. F. Della Salida, *Obbedienza e pace. Il vescovo A. G. Roncalli tra Sofia e Roma (1925–1934)*, Genoa 1988; A. Melloni, *Tra Istanbul, Atene e la guerra. A. G. Roncalli vicario e delegato apostolico 1935–1944*, Genoa 1993.

10. Fouilloux, *Les catholiques et l'unité*; on Roncalli's spirituality, see Melloni, *Il Giornale dell'Anima di Giovanni XXIII*, Milan 2000.

11. Della Salida, *Obbedienza e pace*.

12. Alberigo, *Dalla Laguna al Tevere. A. G. Roncalli da san Marco a san Pietro*, Bologna 2000.

13. V. Martano, *Athenagoras il patriarca (1886–1972). Un cristiano fra crisi di coabitazione e utopia ecumenica*, Bologna 1996, pp.382–3.

14. Ibid., pp.428–30.

15. E. Carpenter, *Archbishop Fisher: His Life and Times*, Norwich 1992, p.737.

16. On the announcement speech see my 'Prodromi e preparazione del discorso d'annuncio del Vaticano II ("Questa festiva Ricorrenza", 25 gennaio 1959)', *Rivista di Storia e Letteratura religiosa* 28 (1992), pp.607–43.

17. *Storia del concilio Vaticano II*, 1, ed Melloni, *L'altra Roma. Politica e S. Sede durante il concilio Vaticano II*, Bologna 2000.

18. P. Duprey, 'Les gestes œcuméniques de Paul VI', *Proche Orient Chrétien* 48 (1978), pp.145–67.

19. Martano, *Athenagoras il patriarca*, p.472.

20. P. Kizeridis, *Il dialogo tra le chiese cattolica romana e ortodossa dal 1920 all'abolizzione delle scomuniche*, Rome 1966, pp.81–3.

21. Transcription from a microphone 'inadvertently' left on, in A. Wenger, *Les trois Rome*, Paris 1991, pp.141–50.

22. Martano, *Athenagoras il patriarca*, pp.473–4.

23. O. Chadwick, *Michael Ramsey: A Life*, Oxford 1991, pp.314–22.

24. Cf. A. Paravicini Bagliani, *Il trono di Pietro. L'universalità del papato da Alessandro III a Bonifacio VIII*, Rome 1996.

25. Wearing these tokens, Montini and Ramsey took part the following day in a joint prayer service at St Paul's without the Walls.

26. *Insegnamenti di Paolo VI*, 13, Rome 1977, p.1516.

27. See, e.g., the acute analysis by A. Maffeis, *Giustificazione*, Brescia 1998.

28. *Cardinal Yves Congar (1904–1995)*, ed A. Vauchez, Paris 1999, pp.117–65.

29. Y. Congar, *Mon Journal du Concile*, 10 July 1963 (mss in Archives du Saulchoir, Paris, and Fondazione per le scienze religiose, Bologna).
30. Cf. N. Vian (ed), *Anni e opere di Paolo VI*, Rome 1978.
31. Congar, *Mon Journal du Concile*, 4 June 1964.
32. *Storia del concilio Vaticano II*, 4.
33. Congar, *Mon Journal du Concile*, 19 November 1964.
34. Ibid., 14 September 1965.
35. This thesis has been partly reconsidered in Duprey (n. 18 above).
36. On the prevalence of gestures in the present pontificate see Alberigo, 'Jean Paul II. Dix ans de pontificat', *Etudes* 368/5 (1988), pp.669–81.
37. Just as in international relations contact between two or more leaders, inside or outside the context of the great supranational organs, has become easier but also less significant: cf. E. Di Nolfo, *Storia delle relazioni internazionali*, Rome-Bari 1994.
38. Cf. G. Ruggieri, 'Il vicolo cieco dell'ecumenismo. A proposito di alcune publicazione recenti', *Cristianesimo nella storia*, 9 (1988), pp.563–615; on the movement see Velati, *Una difficile transizione*.
39. Just as dialogue does, so gesture represents a challenge to the institution: the papacy (which has known how to make gestures, without feeling embarrassed by the anxiety of those who asked what their theology is and saw yawning behind them a geat void inhabited by an unexpected longing for unity) is not yet at ease with encouraging and noticing gestures born out of the actual tissue of life in communities, where it nevertheless asks what their theology is.
40. On the drawing back from the prospect of a shared chalice see Martano, *Athenagoras*, pp.512–16.

The Petrine Ministry as Service of the 'Pilgrim Churches'

GIUSEPPE ALBERIGO

I. The ecclesial context

According to many people in the Christian churches a major change is taking place, though its outlines are still uncertain; one feature of it is a crisis of the credibility, prestige and identity of the Roman papacy.

The emerging characteristic of this complex change is that the churches are seeking to live out their own faithfulness to the gospel. This has to be achieved by a renewal of their internal life and a credible presence among men and women. Underlying this effort is the impulse given by Vatican II and the whole ecumenical movement to a conception of the church which has been stripped of the heavy incrustations imposed over the course of the centuries by Roman law. The prospects of an *aggiornamento* of the papacy have to be seen within the ecclesial situation and in connection with the affirmation of a new image of the church. Any claim to self-sufficiency on the part of the papacy is increasingly leading to isolation, a lack of credibility and rejection.

Nor can the problems of the papacy be contained within the narrow limits of a rationalization aimed at efficiency. We can see that the hoped-for 'internationalization' of the college of cardinals and the Roman Curia has not borne the promised fruit. Nor can we forget that the Roman papacy is a prominent institution, both inside and outside Catholicism, which has not only institutional but also spiritual and theological significance. For at least ten centuries the papacy has been the needle's eye through which many of the major Christian events pass – for better or for worse.

Some options seem to be a precondition of dealing with this problem correctly:

(a) The choice of a papacy which serves the communion and the union between the churches and therefore is an institution which stands between the churches and not above them. In other words the pope is in first place the Bishop of Rome, and it must be realized that any other ministry or service can be fruitful only if it does not imply subordination or, worse, the abdication of the Roman episcopate, but rather is a surplus product of it;

(b) The choice of a papacy which does not believe that it is completely determined or exhaustively expressed by the prerogatives of primacy and infallibility but – also – considers itself to be open to marked changes and capable of new modes of being within the Roman communion and – even more – within the 'Catholic' communion;

(c) The choice of a papacy which refuses to make itself the major centre which rivals and ultimately is on the same level as the great centres of power (the United Nations, superstates, the major economic and financial centres, etc.), i.e. an end to temporalism in all its forms.

(d) Finally, the choice of a papacy which is open to effective collegiality, active and capable of furthering communion and union: a *primus inter pares* and not a superbishop.

On the other hand the renewal of the papacy is not just a matter of debate. In fact the election in 1978 of a Slavonic pope, by interrupting an Italian monopoly which had lasted a century, bore witness to the concrete possibility of innovation. The practice, introduced by John Paul II, of a pope constantly on the move points in the same direction. Now that we have an 'itinerant style' of potentially institutional magnitude which has gone so far as to change the face of relations between the centre and the periphery of the Roman church, the same pattern has also had a tendency to subvert the relationship between the centre and the periphery. Despite the critical reservations about the mode of the journeys (triumphalistic style, prepared speeches, the excessive brevity and the selection of encounters), they must be seen to be important as an embryonic overcoming of Roman centralism. There is a recognition, implicit but transparent, of individual situations in the church, and of how fruitful it can be to confront them and their underlying cultures. So there is no going back on the dialogue about the effective pastoral responsibilities of Peter's successor and the bishops.

The development of *ad limina* visits by the bishops to Rome, organized on the basis of the conferences of bishops (national or regional), which have superseded their traditional individual approaches, have complemented this itinerant style. And finally the periodical sessions of the Synod of Bishops – though largely unsatisfactory – have been a novelty and have caused problems for the customary curial order.

Finally, on an 'external' level, the commitment of John Paul II to the defence and promotion of human rights, even after the disappearance of the Communist regimes, is a relevant example of a 'primatial' initiative carried out with the consensus of the churches, which can truly echo the gospel.

Another significant contribution to this climate of renewal is the affirmation in the Christian traditions which differ from that of Rome of calmer and more constructive attitudes towards the past. The legitimacy of a Petrine succession and its roots in the church of Rome are regarded in a new light. The same goes for the recognition of the opportunities and the fruitfulness of a service of communion between the churches beyond the confines of the Roman Catholic tradition.

II. The varied history of the papacy

From a historical point of view, the existence in various periods of history of remarkably different types of papacy indicates that there is no single and supra-historical 'model'. The papacy has from time to time undergone considerable changes against the background of specific historical circumstances.

The doctrinal definitions of the papacy themselves leave room for change and therefore for effective renewal in the patterns, content and aims of the papal service.[1] In particular the possibility of exercising authority in the universal church by means of an action which is habitually and effectively collegial is crucial. It is also important to rediscover how fruitful doctrinal aspects of the papacy can be which more modern theology has obscured, like the origin and nature of the papal service in the footsteps of Peter and Paul. A greater awareness of the Pauline charisma would open up the way to new enrichments of the image and action of the papacy. On the other hand, the factors which led to a greater rigidity of the papacy are not strictly speaking dogmatic but rather are of an ideological and cultural kind, like the thesis of the papal 'monarchy', introduced from the thirteenth century on.

The strict context of the papal ministry is that of communion between the churches. Therefore a renewal of the papacy necessarily entails a reference to the shared lines of reform of the churches which have been dominant in ecclesial reflection, debate and experience. It would be arbitrary to schematize and generalize, but in fact the ferments of development present in the church are less unitary than ever, though they are more profound in their roots and inspiration. Here change should come about by overcoming the principle of the institutional fixity of the papacy, which has been progressively strengthened in the second millennium.

To the degree that the papacy aspires to be the centre and guarantor of the gospel faith and ecclesial communion, it would seem to be a *conditio sine qua non* that it should accept being institutionally 'itinerant'. Its adaptation to the needs of bearing witness to the faith is the very measure of its authority. Here is an expression of the principle *ecclesia semper reformanda*, according to which no Christian form of institution can be definitive, given that the assimilation to the gospel is never finished and that the service of the pilgrim people of God in history requires the papacy to have an attitude and a disposition which is coherently 'itinerant'.

III. The pope as bishop of the church of Rome

The functions of the pope as Bishop of Rome constitute his original title, not only in a historical sense but also from a theological point of view. It is not 'archaeological' to point out that the effective and responsible leadership by the pope of the church of God which lives in Rome is the first and basic renewal of the papacy. Direct and concrete contact with the problems of Christian life in his community would restore a human face to the pope: as a Christian among Christians and a pastor among pastors.

The content of an orientation of this kind can be indicated only typologically: it would need to emerge from communal reflection of the Roman ecclesial community itself at a spiritual and historical level. This perspective would, for example, facilitate a transparent practice of poverty, which is perhaps the safest criterion of being in accord with the gospel.

The authority of poverty is another very relevant dimension of the papal office. In fact the cultural values and in particular the Christian revelation and the various dogmatic formulations by which the papacy seeks to guarantee and safeguard it have frequently become exorbitant in form and content by comparison with the nucleus which is guaranteed by the Bible. To accept and live out a state of poverty would mean recognizing the inadequacy of the church, and therefore also of the papacy, to live out the gospel, and accepting that often Christians cannot say or do anything when confronted with the problems which face humankind.

A pope who was first of all bishop of Rome would also make a decisive contribution to the problem of election, which otherwise risks becoming increasingly confused. The election of the Bishop of Rome can only take account of his responsibilities for the pilgrim church of God in Rome.

IV. The service of communion

No less relevant is the problem of pontifical service relative to the communion of the churches. In this connection it is necessary to pay very careful attention to some institutional mechanisms which dominate the function of leading the universal church and therefore affect any kind of renewal.[2]

Vatican II has affirmed most explicitly that in the past there has been the possibility of both a collegial and a personal exercise of supreme authority in the church. Just as for centuries there has been a prevalence of the personal exercise of authority, so now a habitually collegial exercise of responsibilities relating to ecclesial communion would seem indispensable. That implies both the creation of an organ capable of ordinarily exercising such responsibilities and a completely new selection of those competences related to responsibility itself, along with an endorsement of other organs concerned with communion, constituted on the basis not only of ministries (the bishops) but also of communities (the churches).

It seems realistic to begin with the relations between the papacy and the synod of bishops.[3] The synod of bishops engages in deliberation and is appointed for a fixed period. That means that the pope should be obligated not to take action on a personal initiative over matters which are within the competence of the synod[4] and should respect its decisions. The decisions of the synod should be the fruit of a synodical dialectic, like that between the pope and the curia. The competence of the synod should relate essentially to communion between the churches at a universal level, according to the maxim *quod omnes tangit, ab omnibus tractari et approbari debet*. That all should discuss and approve what affects all is a maxim which has not been superseded. This could also happen gradually, provided that there were an organic pattern and an explicit will to move in this direction. A progressive extension of deliberative competence would also require the synod to meet at much closer intervals (every six months?) and to determine its own modes of functioning.

It would also be interesting to open up a debate on the composition of the synod. At present it is composed not only of bishops but also of other prelates who have responsibilities in the religious orders or in the Curia. This composition seems to fit in with the Roman tradition and in part with the Orthodox and Anglican tradition; however, it is far removed from the Reformation experience, and above all it pays insufficient respect to a church understood as a people of brothers and sisters, with different and complementary services and charisms. It would be more convincing if the synod tried to respect all of these. Great representativeness would be an important contribution to the realization of 'conciliar praxis', and would constitute an extremely promising perspective for the renewal of the life of the Christian committees and not only of ecclesiastical structures.

Another crucial passage relates to the formation of an executive collegial organ, presided over by the pope, which would be responsible for all current decisions relating to communion among the churches. Because it would necessarily be restricted in membership, it should be characterized not so much by representativeness as by the capacity to achieve an effective circulation of brotherhood in the faith, of aid, and of an exchange of information between the churches, resulting in shared responsibility in the *una sancta* and stimulating contributions in keeping with the gifts of all the members. This collegial organ could have a nucleus – subject to partial periodical renewal – supplemented *ad hoc* by other members, depending on the particular issue (regional areas, specific problems, spiritual traditions). It could perhaps make use of the way in which the consistory of cardinals, presided over by the Bishop of Rome, has functioned for several centuries: it meets almost every six months, examines topics for which one or two members have been previously made responsible, and makes majority decisions, except that the vote of the pope has a particular weighting. Such an organ could meet in different places and should be distinct from the Curia, which would only be its subordinate administrative apparatus. The members would have to come from individual local churches and should return to these at the end of their period of responsibility.

The collegial organs proposed for normative responsibility and the service of communion and unity respectively would be decisively affected by an awareness of the levels on which their work should be focussed and the subjects that it would have to cover.[5]

It would also be necessary to deal with one of the crucial points of the current ecclesiastical system: the centralization of the nomination of bishops in Rome. The jealous claim to these nominations gives the impression that the Bishop of Rome attaches more importance to institutionally guaranteed conformity than to the action of the Spirit and the efficacy of the example of the apostles. The current system should be gradually dismantled, to restore such responsibilities to the ecclesial communities concerned, aided by the sister churches and their bishops. It could prove fruitful to move in experimentally in different directions and also to try out different systems for different geo-cultural areas. In any case it would be important to renew the authority of conferences of bishops or neighbouring bishops to co-opt, also increasing consultative and designatory bodies involving the faithful and interested clergy.

It would also be necessary to confront the complex of problems posed by the Roman Curia. First of all the Christian churches urgently need to become aware that the Curia is a problem for the whole communion of the churches. In fact the only ecclesiologial legitimation that can be given to the Curia is that it is (or should be) a complex of services for the communion of the churches. It is impossible to ignore a potential tension between useful opportunities for common services on the one hand and the accumulation of power which that creates for those who provide the services on the other. The current Curia is the historical and political product of the progressive monarchy at the head of the church. The Curia itself has formed the most refined instrument of the papal monarchy and at the same time perhaps its most effective limit, to the degree that it has shown stubborn resistance to any completely personal government on the part of the pope.

A 'reconversion' of the Curia would seem extremely hard, but if one wanted to introduce a new historical stage of the Petrine ministry, the generative capacity of the new order should provide adequate and coherent instruments, as the mediaeval and modern papacy were able to do in their time. One suggestive possibility would be to entrust services for the communion of the churches to individual local churches in keeping with particular circumstances. This would be an occasion for ecclesial growth which would be assessed according to criteria of ecclesiology and not of efficiency. The Roman church in particular offers the most striking example of a universal ministry entrusted to a local church. Why not endorse this formula by entrusting – perhaps only for limited periods – a universal ministry to an ecclesial community which was effectively responsible for it, as well as offering it material hospitality?[6] This could be an effective way of overcoming the concentration of power, of de-bureaucratizing services and achieving a really inter-cultural status, which would be far more significant than the disappointing internationalization of the Roman Curia. The tenacious viscosity of the Europeanization of Christianity cries out to be overcome at a cultural level, but also at an institutional level.

V. The service of union

The contribution of the papacy towards brotherhood between the churches and their unity calls for a horizontal and no longer a vertical qualification of the relationship between the church of Rome and its bishop and the Christian churches.[7] An analogous action took place – but in the opposite direction – with the Latinization of the Christian East brought about in Rome, above all after the Fourth Crusade, through the absorption of the

Orthodox churches. Overcoming the authority of supremacy and the consequent centralization of power cannot mean dispersion, but polycentrism in respect of all traditions. Research into the much that unites all Christians and emphasis on it should be systematically put before motives of division, however legitimate. It is in connection with this that the efficacy of repentance must be shown, turning upside down the priority given for centuries to differences in favour of a recognition of the common faith.

Ecumenical relations need urgently to move from the level of courtesy to more ecclesial (and less ecclesiastical) levels.[8] It seems vital to move from doctrinal ecumenism to a 'pastoral ecumenism' which is capable of transcending the present impasse in the search for doctrinal agreements. 'Pastoral ecumenism' is called for as commitment to a free and bold search in the perspective of the faith lived out by the ecclesial communities and their capacity to present Christ in a transparent way to the sisters and brothers of the different societies and cultures of today. This involves an attitude which is not focussed on the self but on 'the others', which is already present in so many members of the different 'divided' Christian churches. This attitude is no longer just one of 'dialogue' – which tends to crystallize the diversities – but of a common quest in a context of brotherhood regained.

In particular the preparation and convening of a Christian 'pre-council', i.e. with the active involvement of all the main Christian traditions, seems increasingly desirable. This would be a pre-council aimed at preparing for an 'ecumenical' council which could truly bring together and express the Christian awareness of our times.

There is a further series of points of ecumenical relevance which could profit from actions on the part of the papacy.[9] The question of the nunciatures arises here. Regarded as purely historical and also relatively recent entities (from the end of the fifteenth century), they can be viewed with a certain empiricism. Their significance could well be reduced, making them a sign of union between the episcopates and the governments concerned. Here it is obvious that the functions of nuncio could be entrusted to the primates of each nation. It could be objected that this could lead to the individual national churches finding themselves less supported and protected from political power. In certain circumstances the papacy has in fact exercised the function of safeguarding the churches, but it is necessary to evaluate the ecclesial and spiritual 'cost' of such safeguards.

At all events it should be recognized that at a historical and political level, as at the level of faith, solidarity between the churches seems at least capable of raising up a church which finds itself in difficulties. It would also be worth considering the revival of reciprocal representatives among the major churches, as happened for centuries among the patriarchates with the apocrisarii.

Precisely if one accepts the variability of criteria which have guided the Roman papacy in more recent times, there is a new possibility of formulating orientations and alternative actions which are both concrete and coherent, and perhaps capable of reviving a complex and much discussed historical tradition of leadership.

VI. Some methodological comments

In the best instances, articles like this can feed the debate, by pointing to increasingly diffuse authorities. However, it would be naïve to expect that this could indicate the lines of the hoped-for changes. Reform projects, however authoritative, from St Bernard to Rosmini, have never proved successful.

However, there have been historical circumstances, social conditions, the breath of the Spirit, which have impelled Christianity empirically – and perhaps in a 'disordered' way – to those *aggiornamenti* which no one plans or is capable of bringing about. A marked concern for renewal and a corresponding capacity to obey the Spirit are the indispensable premise for the papacy to change from being the 'major obstacle on the way of ecumenism' to effective service and faith and the communion of the 'pilgrim churches'.

However, the movement of a pope from one to another is usually a crucial moment: here there is change rather than continuity. There are always forces and circumstances which try to stifle this dynamic in the name of continuity, bringing into action strong institutional conditionings and as it were blackmailing the climate of the election and the new person elected. But it is also true that the exceptional nature of circumstances has always got the better of these 'taxidermists', so that neither the choice of the conclave nor the work of the various popes has been conditioned by the presumption of continuity. Moreover, on each occasion the change of pope has indicated a rediscovery of the very broad scope for innovation implicit in the papal institution, which allows each newly-elected pope to give his office a new profile.

Translated by John Bowden

Notes

1. Cf. K. Schatz, *Il primato del papa. La sua storia dalle origini ai giorni nostri*, Brescia 1996.

2. In recent years a number of authoritative treatments of this subject have been published: P. Hünermann (ed), *Papstamt und Ökumene. Zum Petrusdienst und der Einheit aller Getauften*, Regensburg 1997; H. J. Pottmeyer, *Towards a Papacy in Communion: Perspectives from Vatican Councils I & II*, New York 1998; A. Acerbi (ed), *Il ministero del papa in prospettiva ecumenica*, Milan 1999; H. Schütte (ed), *Im Dienst der einen Kirche. Ökumenische Überlegungen zur Reform des Papstamts*, Paderborn 2000; J. R. Quinn, *The Reform of the Papacy. The Costly Call to Christian Unity*, New York 2000; P. Tihon (ed), *Changer la papauté*, Paris 2000. Cf. M. Faggioli, 'Note in margine a recenti contributi per una riforma ecumenica del papato', *Cristianesimo nella Storia* 22, 2001, and also the articles on the same subject by A. Dulles and L. Örsy in *America del 2000*. A revival of attention to the figure of the pope, with real romanticism about imaginary figures of successors to Peter, has also emerged in major literature: cf. above all S. Knecht, *Visione del Papa*, Brescia 1978.

3. Cf. G. Alberigo, 'Istituzioni per la comunione tra l'episcopato universale e il vescovo di Roma', *Cristianesimo nella storia* 2, 1981, pp.235–66.

4. At all events an 'exceptional situation' could come about through anomalous circumstances, as A. Acerbi envisages, but normally the Bishop of Rome should resort to the personal exercise of authority only for the functions which P. Hunermann has acutely described as 'notarial': 'Die Herausbildung der Lehre von den definitiv zu haltenden Wahrheiten seit dem zweiten Vatikanischen Konzil. Ein historischer Bericht und eine systematische Reflexion', *Cristianesimo nella Storia* 21, 2000, pp.71–101.

5. There would be a need to avoid forms of apparent collegiality, occasions on which the church was bureaucratically addressed on such problems so that the final decision could be presented as based on a previous consultation. A proper communion among the churches could be expressed only by means of a dynamic equilibrium of *traditio* and *receptio*. There is a need for an effective readiness to change both subjects of the communion, the giver and the receiver. However, the universalistic ecclesiology has led to this demand being lost sight of, thus exonerating the papacy from an effective exchange with the churches. This authority could also be expressed by means of the 'principle of subsidiarity', but only provided that there was an awareness that in the ecclesial sphere this has a significance only remotely analogous to its meaning in politics and civil life. In an ecclesial context the significance of this principle proves to be quite narrow and is limited by the 'eucharistic' and therefore authentic nature of the local church. It is not a part of the universal church which would be the 'whole'; rather, each church is complete in itself in its essential elements. This implies that what relates to the ecclesial quality (the 'essence') of each church cannot be expropriated or arrogated by other authorities. However, problems common to

several territorial churches can be examined and decided on by common regional, continental or universal organs, not through subsidiarity but through 'communion'.

6. An analogous reference could be made to the decentralization by the United Nations Organization (UNO), which has moved from its seat in New York organizations like UNESCO to Paris, FAO to Rome, IAEA to Vienna, ILO to Geneva, IMO to London and UNEP in Nairobi, to mention only the best known.

7. Paul VI had recognized from 1967 that the pope is 'without doubt the most serious obstacle on the way of ecumenism' (*AAS* 59, 1967, p.497). However, a declaration of such gravity could only be ambivalent, if one thinks of the criteria stated in I Corinthians (1.10–11), according to which the church cannot be divided in the name of any ministry. It follows from this that the situation noted by Paul VI and then again by Jean Paul II is ecclesiologically pathological. The recognition of different degrees in the relationship of the churches with the papacy seems to offer a prospect of overcoming the present impasses which is in keeping with the Christian tradition and with the awareness of the faith of the churches.

8. In 1973 the climate of a renewed commitment to reunion generated the christological agreement on the presence of Christ in the eucharist between Reformed and Lutherans. 1989 saw the agreement between the Orthodox and 'Monophysite' churches on the humanity and the divinity of Christ. The encyclical *Ut unum sint* (1995) has again brought up the possibility of the Roman pontificate being reformulated in a context of union and no longer of controversy. In 1999 the agreement on the doctrine of justification between Catholic and Protestants healed a wounding post-Tridentine controversy. The request for forgiveness made by John Paul II on the threshold of the millennium has opened up important space. In May 2000 the dogged work of Jean Marie Tillard, whose recent death we mourn, led to the meeting of Roman Catholic and Anglican bishops in Toronto.

9. For example a doctrinal declaration which repudiated the doctrine of the two swords, in particular the claims contained in the bull *Unam sanctam*, and which renounced any form of temporalism, even indirect forms.

DOCUMENTATION

Reactions to *Dominus Iesus* in the German-Speaking World

CHRISTINE VAN WIJNBERGEN

On 5 September 2000 the Roman Congregation for the Doctrine of Faith produced a document which has had more repercussions than any papal encyclical of the last twenty years. What was intended by its main author to be a doctrinal climax to the Holy Year has threatened to become a catastrophe for ecumenical relations and inter-faith dialogue. The document concerned is the 'Declaration *Dominus Iesus* on the Unicity and Salvific Universality of Jesus Christ and the Church'. Moreover it can hardly be a coincidence that the declaration was published two days after the beatification of Pius IX.

In addition to an introduction and a conclusion, the document consists of six chapters which reflect consistently on central themes of Christian theology. The areas discussed are: revelation, the incarnate Logos and the Holy Spirit, salvation in Jesus Christ, the kingdom of God and the kingdom of Christ, and the non-Christian religions. Many analyses agree that two issues lie behind *Dominus Iesus*:

(a) The dialogue with the non-Christian religions and the danger of religious relativism detected by the Congregation. To be more specific: the declaration seeks to put an end to developments in the inculturation of theology in Asia and pluralist theologies of religion like those of John Hick and Paul Knitter, which reject the absolute claim of Christianity to truth and think that there are many possible ways to salvation.

(b) The ecumenical movement within Christianity. To be more specific: the declaration rejects a pluralistic ecclesiology according to which the one church of Jesus Christ is realized in the same way in several Christian church communities.

I. Inter-faith dialogue

The original aim of this account was to report the state of discussion on these two questions. That aim has been abandoned. We have had hardly any reactions from the non-European world. There seem to be two reasons for this. First, Roman documents play much less of a role in non-Western cultures than Western theologians often assume. Secondly, the restraint of Christian theologians from Third World countries raises the question whether open reactions are possible at all. After all, in 1997 the Sri Lankan theologian Tissa Balasuriya was excommunicated, and statements by the Indian Jesuit Anthony de Mello were condemned in 1998. The investigation into J. Dupuis, *Toward a Christian Theology of Religious Pluralism* (Mary-knoll 1997), which was completed in January 2001, also raises questions.

One of the few publications which goes into the problem of pluralism is the article by Georg Evers, 'Zu kurz gesprungen? "Dominus Iesus" und die Theologie in Asia', *Herder Korrespondenz* 54, 12/2000, pp.618–24. Dr Evers is associated with the Missio Institute in Aachen.

Evers points out that not only is the Roman declaration damaging to other religions, but in some countries it can also have far-reaching political consequences. For instance, in India the declaration is grist to the mills of radical Hindu groups which accuse Christians of despising other religions and of being the tools of a foreign power.

Evers is indignant about the view of *Dominus Iesus* which is stated quite firmly (no.7), that the difference between 'theologal faith' and the inner convictions of other religions must continue to be maintained. That means that the non-Christian religions are reduced to merely human experiences and have no place in God's plan of salvation. He cites a number of Indian, Vietnamese and Philippine theologians. For Asian theologians, the life and work of Jesus Christ and not the problem of his metaphysical identity stands at the centre of christology. For them Jesus Christ is the definitive, if not the exhaustive, symbol of this world's experience of God. The uniqueness of Jesus does not do away with the value of symbols in the other religions (Michael Amaldadoss).

The question is: what value is to be given to the statements and gestures of the present pope which suggest a more differentiated view of relations with other religions?

II. The ecumenical problem

In Europe, above all in German-language areas, the second question, that of the ecumenical movement within Christianity and the concept of the church, has a central place in the debate. That *Dominus Iesus* has provoked vigorous reactions above all in Germany has to do first with the importance and topicality of ecumenical dialogue there and secondly with the fact that in Germany the declaration has widely been seen as the work of Cardinal Ratzinger himself. Certainly he signed the document as the Prefect of the Congregation of the Doctrine of Faith and not as author, but it is assumed that at all events he is the mind behind it (the *New Catholic Reporter* names as assistant authors the Salesian Fr Angelo Amato, Vice Rector of the Pontifical Salesian University in Rome, and Mgr Fernando, Vicar General of Opus Dei).

German-language reactions to the Roman document have not always been easy to find because many of them have appeared in confessional church periodicals, in a variety of newspapers and also in theological journals. So a recently published collection of German reactions, Michael J. Rainer (ed), *Dominus Iesus*,[1] is of great importance here. The collection begins with the text of *Dominus Iesus* in full (pp.3–28), followed by the text of an interview with Cardinal Ratzinger in the *Frankfurter Allgemeine Zeitung* (pp.29–45).[2] In this interview he confirms a number of statements in the declaration and replies to his first critics.

The book contains contributions (some specially written for it, and others taken from newspapers and periodicals) by authors including Ingolf U. Dalferth, Hermann Häring, Bernard Jochen Hilberath, Maria Jepsen, Eberhard Jüngel, Hans Küng, Robert Leicht, John D'Arcy May, Peter Neuner, Konrad Raiser, Theodor Schneider, Clemens Thoma and Jürgen Werbick. The number of Protestant commentators here is amazingly high. Two articles by the chief Protestant spokesman, Eberhard Jüngel, are included. The volume ends with a very extensive bibliography of critical and supportive commentaries on *Dominus Iesus*.

The main reason for offence is felt to be the exclusive interpretation of a famous statement of Vatican II that the church of Christ 'subsists in' (*subsistit in*)[3] the Catholic church. For historical and systematic-theological reasons this interpretation is generally rejected. It is natural that the reactions from the Reformation side are focussed above all on this point. Ratzinger complains in the *Frankfurter Allgemeine Zeitung* interview (p.30) that the criticism of the document is directed above all at the ecclesiological statements, whereas the congregation was concerned only to make clear the central position of the 'Lord Jesus Christ' in the Christian faith.

Protestant theologians in particular, with the 1934 Barmen Theological Declaration in mind, accept above all the christocentricity of *Dominus Iesus*, but reject its ecclesiological conclusions. The fact that there is no agreement in any way between the context of the two documents (the 1934 text was meant above all to make clear that no other authority – Führer, state or political party – than that of Jesus Christ was to be accepted) is left out of account. Eberhard Jüngel ('Quo vadis Ecclesia', pp.59–67 and 'Paradox Ökumene', pp.68–78)[4] also sees an agreement between the christocentric revelation theology of the Barmen Declaration and the christological statements of the Roman document. Moreover he thinks that the Vatican II assertion, repeated by *Dominus Iesus*, that elements of sanctification and truth can also be found outside the Catholic Church, is compatible with what Karl Barth, the author of the Barmen Theological Declaration, said in a later commentary, namely that the unicity of Jesus Christ must not be interpreted strictly in exclusive terms: even outside the church and manifest Christianity, likenesses to the kingdom of heaven can be discovered.

Jüngel says that the difficulties within Christianity begin only with the ecclesiological statements of the Roman declaration. He disputes the exclusivist interpretation of the expression '*subsistit in*'. Instead he presents an analogy from trinitarian theology, namely that the subsistence of the church of Jesus Christ in a concrete visible church must be understood in analogy to the subsistence of the one divine being in the three persons of the Father, Son and the Spirit. It follows from this that all Christian churches are representatives of the church of Jesus Christ in the same way as the Catholic church.

In his article 'DOMINUS IESUS. Katholisch – mit Angst vor der Vielfalt?' (pp.144–65), Hermann Häring demonstrates that the ecclesiological statements in *Dominus Iesus* are closely connected with the fundamental and dogmatic theological standpoints in the first three chapters of the document. In the first part of his article he shows that the work must be understood in the light of Ratzinger's theological thought, which has remained consistent over the years. Central to that thought is the normative significance of the theology of the first five centuries. The embedding of Christianity in Greek metaphysical thought has helped Christianity to arrive at its concept of truth.

Häring is opposed to the way in which this document ties christology closely to the interpretations of the early church and makes christology and ecclesiology parallel: in other words to the way in which the unicity and salvific universality of Jesus Christ is transferred to the church and from there to the Catholic church. He sees the ecumenical scandal not so much in the fourth chapter on the church as in the christological thought in the first three chapters. In the last section of his article Häring discusses the concept of truth in *Dominus Iesus*. He criticizes the view of the Congregation of the Doctrine of Faith that the truth is set down in one language, one system of philosophical or symbolic thought, and is the possession of one institution. A static concept of identity goes with this conception of truth. And that leads to fear of a loss of identity. However, scholarly investigations in the last century have shown that identity is not static but has an open character, is a process. That has made it possible to understand religious identity as an ongoing process of identification.

Häring concludes his article with eleven theses in which he once again succinctly sums up the scholarly and pastoral objections. In no. 11, by way of a conclusion he argues that the Congregation for the Doctrine of Faith should have a ten-year silence imposed on it for reflection and conversion.

The underlying concept of truth in *Dominus Iesus* is the central theme of the article by Ferdinand Kerstiens, 'Von der Hoffungsstruktur der Wahrheit' (pp.260–70, originally published in *Orientierung* 64/2000). He points out the linguistic affinities between this document and the *Syllabus Errorum* of the recently beatified Pius IX: the *Syllabus* sums up the untruths which must be rejected; *Dominus Iesus* states not only untruths but the truths which people 'must firmly believe'. Behind these documents is the view that truths and untruths can be fixed in statements without going back to their context in argumentation and culture. Kerstiens compares this approach with the plurality of the Bible, the different christologies of the Gospels and in particular with the notion of truth in the Gospel of John. The truth is not so much a matter of statements but of actions; the truth has to be done (John 3.21).

The collection published by Lit-Verlag is largely about the ecumenical movement within Christianity; the relationship with the world religions, the problem of the claim of Christianity to absoluteness and so on are touched on only in summary fashion. Reflection here is only beginning and must be deepened in the future. A further collection of articles could be devoted to this.

III. Conclusions

In this report it is impossible to quote all the reactions at length. Of course there are also some reactions which explicitly support the tenor of *Dominus*

Iesus.[5] Some professional theologians endorse *Dominus Iesus* as a clear witness to Christ. Here they agree with many Protestant reactions. The strategy of a cautious defence can be detected in the German bishops Kasper (who is now a cardinal) and Lehmann. But such reactions are in the minority.

It seems legitimate to conclude that the attempt of the Congregation of the Doctrine of Faith to secure the unicity and salvific universality of the Christian religion and the (Catholic) Church once and for all has largely failed. However, for the moment the discussion risks taking two divergent courses. One is the growing recognition of the non-Christian religions as ways to God; the other is the abiding conviction that salvation for the world has been attained through Christ alone. Probably even Catholic theology cannot sustain this division between religious openness and soteriological exclusiveness.

Translated by John Bowden

Notes

1. Michael J. Rainer (ed), *Dominus Iesus. Anstössige Wahrheit oder anstössige Kirche? Dokumente, Hintergründe, Standpunkte und Folgerungen*, Münster: Lit-Verlag 2000.
2. *Frankfurter Allgemeine Zeitung*, 22 September 2000.
3. *Lumen gentium*, 8.
4. 'Quo vadis Ecclesia' appeared in *Deutsches Allgemeines Sonntagsblatt* of 15 September 2000 under the title 'Nur Wahrheit befreit'; 'Paradoxe Ökumene' in *Zeitzeichen* 1, November 2000.
5. Gerhard Lohfink, Arnold Stötzel, Ludwig Weimer, 'Die Stunde der Kirche – Was nach der Erklärung "Dominus Iesus" anders ist', in *Heute im Kirche und Welt. Blätter zur Unterscheidung des Christlichen*, 3 October 2000. See also W. Beinert, *Mittelbayerische Zeitung*, 21 September 2000.

Contributors

JOSÉ OSCAR BEOZZO was born in Santa Adelia (SP), Brazil, in 1941, and ordained priest in the diocese of Lins in 1964. He studied philosophy in São Paulo, theology at the Gregorian University in Rome, and sociology and social communication at the Catholic University of Louvain. He is executive secretary of CESEP (Ecumenical Centre for Services to Evangelization and Popular Education), a member of the executive board of CEHILA (Commission for Study of Church History in Latin America) and a lecturer at the theology faculty of São Paulo University. His publications include *Trabalho, crime e alternativas* (1995); *Igreja no Brasil: de João XXIII a João Paulo II* (1995); and, as editor for the Brazil area, *Historia do Cancilio Vaticano II* (1995).

Address: Rua Oliveira Alves 164, São Paulo (SP) 04210-060, Brazil.
Email: jbeozzo@ax.apc.org

GIUSEPPE RUGGIERI teaches fundamental theology at the Studio Teologico S Paolo di Catania; he is a member of the editorial boards of *Cristianesimo nella storia* and *Concilium*. Recent publications include: *La compagnia della fede, Linee di teologia fondamentale*, Turin 1980; *Fede e cultura* (with I. Mancini), Turin 1979.

Address: Villaggio S Agata Zona B 26 B, 95121 Catania, Italy.
Email: rotger@usa.net

DIMITRI SALACHAS is Professor of Eastern Canon Law in Rome.

Address: Via del Babuino 149, 00187 Rome, Italy
Email: salachas@pcn.net

HANS-JOACHIM SCHULZ was born in 1932 and studied in Rome, in Innsbruck where he was a pupil of Karl Rahner and Josef Andreas Jungmann, and later in Münster. He was ordained priest in Aachen in 1956. From 1965 to 1978 he was Professor of Liturgy in Königstein in the Taunus and in Bochum and from 1978 to 1997 Professor of the History of the Eastern Churches and Ecumenical Theology in Würzburg. His most important books are: *Die byzantinische Liturgie. Glaubenszeugnis und Symbolgestalt*, Trier 1980, 2000; *Die apostolische Herkunft der Evangelien. Zum Ursprung der Evangelienform in der urgemeindlichen Paschafeier*, Quaestiones Disputatae 145, Freiburg 1993; *Bekenntnis statt Dogma. Kriterien der Verbindlichkeit kirchliche Lehre*, Quaestiones Disputatae 163, Freiburg 1966.

Address: Am Kapellenberg 3, D-97332 Volkach-Gaibach, Germany.

ANGELO DI BERARDINO studied at the universities of Valladolid, Vienna, Paris and Naples, ultimately gaining a doctorate in theology, and of Bari and Rome, where he gained a doctorate in history and philosophy. Since 1972 he has been Professor of Patrology at the Augustinianum Patristic Institute in Rome. He is a member of the Centre of Theological Inquiry in Princeton and from 1984 to 2000 was General Secretary of the International Association of Patristic Studies; he is now President. He has written various articles and books; in particular he has edited a three-volume Dictionary of Patristics and Early Christianity and a continuation of Quasten's Patrology. He has also written a history of theology in the patristic period. His main interest is in the institutions of the early church.

Address: Augustinianum, Via Paolo VI 25, 00193 Roma, Italy.
E-mail: preside_ipa@aug.org

OTTO HERMANN PESCH, a Catholic, is Emeritus Professor of Systematic Theology and Controversial Theology in the Faculty of Protestant Theology of the University of Hamburg. He is a specialist in mediaeval theology, above all on Thomas of Aquinas in comparison with the theology of Martin Luther, and on questions of contemporary fundamental theology and dogmatics. At the same time he writes on the communication of faith and spirituality. His books include *Das Zweite Vatikanische Konzil*, Würzburg ⁴2001, and a commentary on the doctrine of sin in Thomas Aquinas, Vol.12 of the German edition of Thomas.

Address: c/o Concilium.

ALPHONSE BORRAS was born in Liège in 1951, and ordained priest in that diocese in 1976. He has a licentiate in theology and a doctorate in canon law from the Gregorian University and is now director of studies at the episcopal seminary of Liège, where he teaches fundamental theology, ecclesiology and canon law. He is Professor of Canon Law at the Catholic University of Louvain and also in charge of the course on penal law in the Department of Canon Law of the Catholic University of Central Africa in Yaoundé, Cameroon. In addition to his works on canon penal law he has written a study of the parish: *Les Communautés paroissiales. Droit canonique et perspectives pastorales*, Paris 1996. He has edited a composite work on lay ministries, *Des laics en responsabilité pastorale? Accueillir de nouveaux ministères*, Paris 1998, and with B. Piottier has written *La grâce du diaconat. Questions actuelles autour du diaconat Latin*, Brussels 1998, together with a number of articles on canon law and pastoral theology. His *Les 'nouveaux ministères'. Accompagner le people de Dieu dans sa mission* is forthcoming, Brussels 2002.

Address: Rue de Prémontré 40, B 4000 Liège, Belgium.

PIERRE VALLIN was born in 1928. Since 1964 he has been Professor of History and Dogmatic Theology, first at the Jesuit Faculty of Lyons, and then, from 1974, at the Centre Sèvres in Paris. He has been co-editor of the journals *Études* and *Recherches de Science Religieuse* (for which he writes the bulletin on ecclesiology). His main publications are: *Le travail et les travailleurs dans le monde chrétien* (1983); *Les chrétiens et leur histoire (1985); Histoire politique des chrétiens* (1988). He has written for *Le Canon des Écritures*, ed C. Theobald (1990), and contributed articles on the Jesuits, Prophecy and Work to the *Dictionnaire de Spiritualité*.

Address: Centre Sèvres, 35bis rue de Sèvres, 75006 Paris, France.

FAUSTINO TEIXERA was born in Juiz de Fora in Matto Grosso, Brazil in 1954. A lay theologian, he studied philosophy, science of religion and theology. He lectured at the Pontifical University in Rio de Janeiro for four years, and he obtained a doctorate in dogmatic theology from the Gregorianum in 1985, with a thesis on the base church communities in Brazil. Since 1989 he has been an Assistant Professor in Science of Religions at the federal university of Juiz de Fora. His publications include: *A gênese das CEBs no Brasil* (1988); *A espiritualidade do seguimento* (1994); *Teologia das religiões: uma visão panorâmica* (1995); *Os encontros intereclesiais de CEBs no Brasil* (1996).

ALBERTO MELLONI gained a degree in history at the University of Bologna and a doctorate in the history of religion in 1988. He has been a visiting fellow at the Catholic University of Fribourg, Switzerland, and since 1994 has taught history at the University of Rome (Roma 3). He is member of the Institute of Religious Studies and on the boards of the John XXIII Foundation for Religious Studies, Bologna and *Cristianesimo nella storia*. He has written and edited several books on John XXIII (*A. G. Roncalli-Giovanni XXIII, Il giornale dell'Anima*, Bologna 1987; *Tra Istanbul, Atene e la guerra. A. G. Roncalli vicario e delegato apostolico 1935–1944*, Genoa 1993; *La predicazione ad Istanbul*, Florence 1994) and is editor of the Italian edition of the History of the Second Vatican Council, directed by G. Alberigo.

Address: Via Crispi 6, I-42100 Reggio Emilia, Italy
Email: Alberto.melloni@tin.it

GIUSEPPE ALBERIGO was born in Varese in 1926. From 1967 he has been Professor of Church History at the University of Bologna and is editor of the quarterly *Cristianesimo nella Storia*. His publications include *Cardinalato e collegialità*, 1969; *Chiesa Conciliare* (1981); *Giovanni XXIII. Profezia nella fedeltà*, 1978; *La réception de Vatican II*, 1985; *La chiesa nella storia*, 1989. He is also editor of the *History of the Second Vatican Council*, published in five volumes and six languages.

Address: Via G. Mazzini 82, I-40138 Bologna, Italy.

CHRISTINE VAN WIJNBERGEN studied French literature at the Sorbonne and history (ancient and mediaeval) at the universities of Utrecht and Nijmegen. At present she is studying theology in Nijmegen. With Hartmut Zapp she has produced the *Verzeichnis kanonistischer Handschriften in den Niederlanden* (Forschungen zur Kirchenrechtswissenschaft, Bd. 3, Würzburg 1988). She is executive secretary of *Concilium*.

Address: Erasmusplein 1, 6525 HT Nijmegen, The Netherlands.
Email: concilium@theo.kun.nl

CONCILIUM

Concilium Subscription Information

Issues to be published in 2001

February	2001/1: *God: Experience and Mystery* edited by Werner Jeanrond and Christoph Theobald
April	2001/2: *The Return of the Just War* edited by María Pilar Aquino and Dietmar Mieth
June	2001/3: *The Oecumenical Constitution of Churches* edited by Oscar Beozzo and Giuseppe Ruggieri
October	2001/4: *Islamophobia* edited by Elisabeth Schüssler Fiorenza and Karl-Josef Kuschel
December	2001/5: *Globalization and its Victims* edited by Jon Sobrino and Felix Wilfred

New subscribers: to receive *Concilium 2001* (five issues) anywhere in the world, please copy this form, complete it in block capitals and send it with your payment to the address below.

Please enter my subscription for Concilium 2001

☐ Individual **£25.00**/*US$50.00*   ☐ Institutional **£35.00**/*US$75.00*

Issues are sent by air to the USA; please add £10/US$20 for airmail dispatch to all other countries (outside Europe).

☐ I enclose a cheque payable to SCM-Canterbury Press Ltd for £/$ ....

☐ Please charge my MasterCard/Visa   Expires ....

............................/.............................../.............................../...........................

Signature ....

Name/Institution ....

Address ....

....

....

Telephone ....

Concilium   SCM Press   9–17 St Albans Place   London N1 0NX   England
Telephone (44) 20 7359 8033   Fax (44) 20 7359 0049
E-mail: scmpress@btinternet.com